THE TURN TO EXPERIENCE IN CONTEMPORARY THEOLOGY

by
Donald L. Gelpi, S.J.

PAULIST PRESS
New York/Mahwah, N.J.

Library of Congress Cataloging-in-Publication Data

Gelpi, Donald L., 1934-
    The turn to experience in contemporary theology / by Donald L. Gelpi.
        p.   cm.
    Includes bibliographical references and index.
    ISBN 0-8091-3452-7 (pbk.)
    1. Experience (Religion) 2. Experience. 3. Theology—20th century. I. Title.
BR110.G45   1994
248.2'01—dc20   93-38868
                                                                    CIP

Published by Paulist Press
997 Macarthur Boulevard
Mahwah, New Jersey 07430

Printed and bound in the
United States of America

Contents

Preface: The Turn to Experience

One often hears systematic theologians talking about the different "turns" contemporary speculative theology has taken. Josiah Royce observed earlier in this century that Christianity has developed as a religion in search of a metaphysics. I believe that Royce has the right of it. Hence, I find it no surprise that many of theology's "turns" correspond to the discovery of new philosophical underpinnings for systematic theological thinking. One therefore hears theologians reflecting on "the turn to the subject" or on "the linguistic turn" in theology.

I would like to call attention in this study to another "turn" that contemporary theological thinking has taken. I refer to "the turn to experience." One finds this particular speculative turn most obviously in the writings of process theologians, who tend on the whole to endorse Alfred North Whitehead's attempt to transform "experience" into a metaphysical category; but one finds the turn to experience surfacing in other areas of contemporary theology as well. The turn to experience characterizes recent attempts to develop what Bernard Lonergan has called a foundational theology of conversion. Among liberation theologians, one finds the turn to experience implicit in Clodovis Boff's attempt to lay epistemological foundations for liberation theology's political preoccupations. One also finds the turn to experience implicit in Cornel West's recent endorsement of prophetic pragmatism; for every version of pragmatism builds on a construct of experience. Moreover, in Edward Schillebeeckx's monumental scholarly attempt to lay New Testament foundations for a speculative Christology, the turn to experience shows up even in the work of a continental European theologian.

Any discussion of a theological turn to experience must, in all honesty, begin by admitting that the term "experience" enjoys a cer-

1

tain pride of place among the weasel words of the English language. Weasel words twist and wriggle. No sooner does one think that one has pinned a weasel word down to a single meaning than one finds it signifying something totally different. The following menu of some of the more common technical and non-technical meanings of "experience" illustrates what I mean by a weasel word.

In non-technical parlance, "experience" often means the kind of practical wisdom that comes from more or less long-term exposure to some reality, mode of procedure, or problem. We find this use of the term, for example, in the phrase: "Only experienced personnel need apply" or in the response "What you say does (or does not) correspond to my experience."

One finds philosophers using the term both broadly and narrowly. Some thinkers, for example, would restrict the term "experience" to the kind of knowledge yielded by what medieval philosophers called "the powers of sense": namely, to the five external senses, proprio-sensation, emotion, imagination, and sense judgments.

Other philosophers contrast experience with understanding, judgment, and decision. "Experience" in this sense of the term designates all uncritical cognition. As soon as one reflects critically on experience, it ceases to qualify as experience and becomes first understanding, then judgment, then decision. In this construct of experience, however, understanding, judgment, and decision sublate experience by turning it into something else[1]

A third philosophical understanding of "experience" broadens the term still further by contrasting the "what" of experience with its "how" and by equating the meaning of "experience" with the latter. In other words, this construct of "experience" extends the term to include the entire spectrum of human evaluative responses. "Experience" thus understood includes sensations, emotions, imagination, judgments of feeling, hypothetical rational inferences, deductions, and the inductive validation or invalidation of deductive predictions.[2]

The broadest use of the term "experience" includes both the what and the how of knowing. In this use of experience, therefore, what one experiences stands within experience, not outside of it. As a consequence, what one experiences helps define the character of any particular instance of experience. Needless to say, in this broadest understanding of experience, the way one experiences, one's evaluative responses to what one experiences, also stands within experience and gives each instance of experience a how. Moreover, the inclusion of both the what and the how in the meaning of the term "experience" allows one to transform it into a metaphysical category, universally applicable in intent.[3]

Speculative debate over the existence and function of unconscious evaluations endows experience with two other possible meanings. Some hard-nosed empiricists would restrict the term "experience" to conscious cognition, while psychoanalytic literature extends the term to include both pre-conscious and unconscious evaluative responses.

Finally, one finds no philosophical consensus concerning the kinds of generic variables that function in human experience. In the philosophical literature, one finds both di-polar and triadic constructs of experience. Schillebeeckx, for example, opts for a di-polar construct of experience. A di-polar construct describes experience as the subjective interrelation of concrete percepts and abstract concepts. A triadic construct portrays experience as a social process which in its higher exemplifications exhibits three different kinds of relational variables: evaluations, actions, and tendencies.

In the chapters that follow I shall attempt to deal in one way or other with all of the foregoing philosophical constructs of experience. In the course of reflecting on their truth and adequacy, I shall attempt to argue that the turn to experience in contemporary theology has yielded mixed and often negative results, and for two reasons. First, contemporary theologians who have attempted the turn to experience have tended to espouse an indefensible, nominalistic, di-polar construct of experience. Such a construct cannot explain even ordinary human social experience, much less the graced transformation of natural human experience by Christian faith. Second, those theologians attempting the turn to experience who manage to avoid the Scylla of nominalism fall into the Charybdis of Kantian logic and of other indefensible aspects of Kantian epistemology.

In the course of my argument I shall also attempt to show that

the theological turn to experience need not endorse these philosophical fallacies. I shall also argue that its failure to date has
resulted from the fact that most of those who have attempted the
turn to experience have, for one reason or another, ignored the
debate about the structure of experience in classical North
American philosophy. That debate engaged some of the giants of
the American religious philosophical tradition: Charles Sanders
Peirce, William James, Josiah Royce, George Santayana, and
Alfred North Whitehead.

In what follows I shall have occasion to refer repeatedly to
the philosophical "realism" of Charles Peirce and to contrast it
with what he called "nominalism." Let me, then, attempt to clarify
what these terms meant to Peirce and what they shall mean for me.

Peirce studied the great medieval thinkers. He found "their
analyses of thought and their discussions of all those questions of
logic that almost trench upon metaphysics...very instructive."[4]
Peirce confessed that the realism of John Duns Scotus had especially influenced his own thinking.[5] Peirce described the issue
between nominalism and realism in the following terms: the two
schools of thought disagree about "whether laws and general types
are figments of the mind or are real."[6] Realists defend the reality of
laws and of generality; nominalists deny it.

Peirce spoke of two kinds of nominalism. Nominalists in the
strict sense of the term "recognize but one mode of being, the
being of an individual thing or fact, the being which consists in the
object's crowding out a place for itself in the universe, so to speak,
and reacting by brute force or fact against all other things."[7] Strict
nominalists hold that a "general rule is nothing but a mere word or
couple of words."[8]

Peirce, however, discerned a second species of nominalism,
which he called "conceptualism." He situated this second form of
nominalism between strict nominalism and realism. The conceptu-
alist recognizes the reality of universals but allows them only the
reality of thought. Conceptualists look upon the laws of nature as
the result of thinking, not as realities in nature itself.[9] In the last
analysis, Peirce regarded nominalism and conceptualism as "essen-

tially the same thing," since both positions rule out in principle the reality of general tendencies in nature.[10]

With this understanding of nominalism in mind, Peirce did not hesitate to classify Descartes, Locke, Berkeley, Hume, Reid, Leibniz, and Kant all as nominalists. He regarded Hegel as a nominalist with realistic yearnings. He felt he could extend the list. In fact, he regarded the whole of post-Cartesian, western philosophy as nominalistic: "Thus, in one word, all modern philosophy of every sect has been nominalistic."[11]

To the doctrine of nominalism, Peirce opposed his form of realism, what he called his doctrine of the three modes of being. He regarded actuality as the most obvious mode of being. It consists of something happening then and there. Actuality takes the form of brute force, of actions and reactions that endow experience with concreteness, with a sense of "thisness." Peirce called this mode of being "secondness" and contrasted it with what he called "firstness" and "thirdness." He correlated the being of firstness with pure possibility. Firstness enjoys particularity, is "something positive and **sui generis**."[12] By thirdness, Peirce meant real generality, the real tendency to react or to respond in a specific way under specifiable conditions. He calls such tendencies laws and insisted that only their reality, their real presence in things, makes scientific thinking possible.[13]

Peirce's triadic metaphysics found an anticipation in his triadic phenomenology of experience. We experience firstness as qualities, or particular evaluative responses; secondness as facts, or concrete actions; and thirdness as laws, or real tendencies.[14]

In what follows, when I use the terms "nominalism" and "realism," I shall employ them in Peirce's understanding of those terms. By nominalism, then, I shall mean any denial of real generality in things. I shall regard the reduction of real generality to subjective concepts, what Peirce calls "conceptualism," as a species of nominalism. I shall, therefore, refer paradoxically on occasion to "Platonic nominalism."

Since Plato stands as the prototypical philosophical realist, the very phrase "Platonic nominalism" will sound, on first hearing, like a contradiction in terms. Platonic nominalists differ, however, from Plato by espousing a form of conceptualism, in Peirce's sense of that term. They reduce the realm of essences (the contemporary Platonic counterpart to Plato's realm of forms) to subjective conceptual feelings at the same time that they equate the physical with the concrete, the sensible, the determinate. I shall argue that Santayana's mature philosophy exemplifies a species of Platonic nominalism as does the Platonism of Alfred North Whitehead.

Moreover, in what follows, I shall espouse a Peircean realism and endorse his triadic construct of experience over against a series of di-polar models of experience that, in my judgment, exemplify what Peirce calls conceptual nominalism. Here, however, one needs to note that Peirce redefined the meaning of realism, just as he redefined the meaning of nominalism. Classical Platonic realism reifies essences, or forms, and locates them in a realm of being that transcends space and time. Peirce regarded what classical Platonism calls "forms" as "qualities," i.e. as particular evaluative responses abstracted both from the realities and actualities they disclose and from the one to whom they disclose them. Peircean realism, then, avoids the essence fallacy. It does not find essences existing in their own right whether in concrete sensible things or in some transcendent Platonic realm. At the same time, Peircean realism asserts the presence in things of laws, of habitual tendencies to act or respond in specific ways and under specifiable circumstances. Moreover, Peircean realism defends the mind's ability to grasp those laws rationally and inferentially.

In other words, in endorsing realism Peirce also reformulated it in ways that, in his judgment, reconciled realism and contemporary scientific modes of thinking. In what follows I shall have occasion to reflect on how Peirce justified that reconciliation. Here it suffices to alert the reader to the different senses in which I shall use the terms "nominalism" and "realism" in the reflections that follow.

Notes

[1] Bernard Lonergan uses the term "experience" in both of these senses: as sensory cognition and as all knowledge prior to critical reflection upon

it. Cf. Bernard Lonergan, **Insight: A Study of Human Understanding** (New York: Philosophical Library, 1958), pp. 271-347; **Method in Theology** (New York: Herder and Herder, 1972), pp. 3-25.

[2] One finds this notion of "experience" in the philosophy of John Dewey; cf. John Dewey, **Experience and Nature** (New York: Dover Publications, 1958), pp. 1-39.

[3] Alfred North Whitehead uses experience in this sense; cf. Alfred North Whitehead, **Process and Reality**, edited by David Ray Griffin and Donald W. Sherburne (New York: Free Press, 1963), p. 167.

[4] Charles Sanders Peirce, **Collected Papers**, edited by Charles Hartshorne and Paul Weiss (8 vols.; Cambridge: Harvard University Press, 1931ff), 1.16.

[5] **Ibid.**, 1.6.

[6] **Ibid.**, 1.16.

[7] **Ibid.**, 1.21.

[8] **Ibid.**, 1.26.

[9] **Ibid.**, 1.27.

[10] **Ibid**.

[11] **Ibid.**, 1.19.

[12] **Ibid.**, 1.25.

[13] **Ibid.**, 1.26.

[14] **Ibid.**, 5.53-65.

1

Schillebeeckx and the Turn to Experience

(I)

Edward Schillebeeckx made his turn to experience in attempting to lay New Testament foundations for a systematic Christology. In this chapter, I shall attempt to assess the speculative results of Schillebeeckx's effort in this regard.

My argument divides into three parts. In the first part, I shall present as clearly and as accurately as I can what Schillebeeckx seems to mean by the term "experience." In the second part, I shall reflect on some of the more obvious inadequacies in this philosophical construct of experience. In the third part of my argument, I shall examine the way in which those inadequacies seriously skew Schillebeeckx's reading of New Testament Christology.

Schillebeeckx defines "experience" as "learning through direct contact with people and things. It is the ability to assimilate perceptions."[1] In other words, one derives perceptions from direct contact with people and things. Assimilation here means conceptual interpretation. Hence, experience correlates concrete perceptions with abstract conceptions.

The assimilation of perceptions places interpretation at the heart of Schillebeeckx's notion of experience. Interpretation constitutes an experience by coloring one's sense of the past, present, and future; for human experience exhibits a temporal structure. Every experience inherits from the past and projects plans for the future. Some elements of interpretation arise from within an experience, other elements enter experience from outside it. Linguistic and social conditioning exemplify elements that enter an experience "from the outside." The fact that an experience has an inside and an outside implies the radical finitude of human experience. Finitude implies fallibility. Human experience always involves guesses, hypotheses, theorizing. When a finite experience meets with resistance to its expectations, it takes on a dialectical character.[2] Moreover, the fact that experiences have insides and outsides means that for Schillebeeckx the experiential assimilation of perceptions transpires within subjectivity.

For Schillebeeckx, the communicability of an experience presupposes its interpreted character. We must deal not only with personal interpretations of experience but with interpretations made by others. Our bodies insert us into environments. As a consequence, not only do we think in a socially conditioned manner, but society can define our very identity as persons.[3]

Traditions hand down interpretations of experience. Experiences that seek to manipulate other experiences claim an authoritative character. Some experiences call others into question; but the authoritarian attempt to rule out new experiences forfeits moral authority through its appeal to coercion. Because the human attempt to assimilate new experiences always labors under the constraints of finitude and fallibility, it always succeeds only more or less.[4]

Schillebeeckx criticizes Immanuel Kant for having defended a closed, individualistic construct of experience that inoculated it against any social influence. Schillebeeckx has read enough social psychology to see through such Kantian solipsism. He insists therefore that we replace a "closed" Kantian interpretation of experience with a socially conditioned one.[5]

In other respects, however, Schillebeeckx's construct of experience acquiesces in many of the presuppositions of Kantian epistemology. Like Kant, for example, Schillebeeckx defends a di-polar construct of experience. Experience has a concrete perceptual pole and an abstract, conceptual, interpretative pole.[6] In the third volume of his study, Schillebeeckx equates the perceptual pole of experience with praxis and the conceptual pole with thought.[7]

Moreover, like Kant, Schillebeeckx seems to acquiesce in a British empiricist interpretation of the perceptual pole of experience. He does so out of the conviction that "the empirical **a priori** of science and technology" has replaced "the religious **a priori**" in modern culture.[8]

Moreover, Schillebeeckx equates the empirical and perceptual with the historical and thus endows both perception and history with concrete facticity.[9] Praxis, the concrete deeds that make up history, provides experience with its objects for interpretation, while interpretation provides experience with its subjective pole.[10]

Schillebeeckx acknowledges two ways of interpreting experience: reason and faith. Like reason, faith offers a theoretical interpretation of praxis.[11] Reason, however, operates autonomously according to the principles of empirical scientific method and of historical-critical method, while faith offers an interpretation of the depth dimension of revelatory experiences. Moreover, that interpretation derives from the inspiration of the Holy Spirit.[12] Faith, then, offers a theoretical account of the meaning of a particular praxis of liberation and redemption.[13] Schillebeeckx finds an unbridgeable gulf dividing the language of reason from the language of faith, and vice versa, although he concedes a legitimacy to both ways of thinking.[14]

The spirit of Kantianism also surfaces in Schillebeeckx's account of the way that God functions within human religious experience. Because faith interprets concretely sensible, empirical realities, Schillebeeckx rules out any possibility of a "supernatural" encounter with God.[15] By "supernatural" Schillebeeckx would seem to mean an encounter with God that occurs with no reference to concrete, sensible facts or outside of an historically developing experience. Schillebeeckx also rules out the possibility of discovering God through "inwardness."[16] We cannot demonstrate the existence of God because the divine transcendence places God beyond the pale of scientific observation and experiment. As a consequence, we encounter God within human experience apophatically, as a limit concept, as an "unknown X" that eludes definition by image and concept.[17] Paradoxically, however, Schillebeeckx holds that we must encounter this utterly transcendent God, this absolute limit of thought and conception, in some concrete, sensible perception.[18] Schillebeeckx, then, would seem to concede to Kant that without some kind of empirical grounding, the concept of "God"

remains empty. At the same time Schillebeeckx fails to explain
how any empirical content can fill the concept of "God" defined as
absolute limit. Indeed, what Schillebeeckx has to say about religious experience leaves me wondering whether the logic of his
position does not force one to espouse a Tillichian theology of
symbol in which spatio-temporal realities can only point to an inef-
fable, transcendent deity but can never in any way express the reality of that deity.

(II)

I have just sketched what Schillebeeckx has to say about
experience. In the present section, I shall examine four of the more
obvious limitations of his notion of experience: 1) its di-polarity;
2) its acquiescence in an empiricist interpretation of the perceptual
pole of experience; 3) its inability to interpret adequately human
religious experience; and 4) its narrow rationalism. As we shall
see, these four inadequacies all imply one another.

In the bibliography that precedes Schillebeeckx's initial discussion of the term "experience" in the second volume of his
Christology, one finds no references to the extensive debate about
the structure and dynamics of experience that one finds in classical
American philosophy.[19] In one sense, I find the omission odd, especially since a growing focus on experience marks one of the distinguishing traits of philosophical thinking in this country. On the
other hand, given the traditional obtuseness of continental
European thinkers when it comes to dealing with American philosophy, perhaps the omission should come as no great surprise.

Nevertheless, a careful study of the debate among American
philosophers about the di-polar vs. the triadic structure of experience would have helped Schillebeeckx avoid some important false
philosophical moves. This debate engaged some of the giants of
the American philosophical tradition; William James, George
Santayana, and Alfred North Whitehead each defended some version of a di-polar construct. Charles Sanders Peirce, the mature
Josiah Royce, and, to a certain extent, John Dewey[20] each defended
the triadic construct.

In **The Problem of Christianity**, Royce, building on Peirce's insights, formulated perhaps the most devastating criticism one can make of a di-polar construct of experience. If experience consists only in the interrelation within subjectivity of concrete percepts with abstract concepts, as the di-polar construct holds, then one cannot account philosophically for the social character of knowing. Why? Because if the subjective interrelation of percepts and concepts provides an exhaustive definition of human cognition, then all knowledge takes place exclusively between one's ears. In other words, the di-polar interpretation of experience transforms it into such a purely subjective process that, as a construct, lacks the categories to interpret the basic human experience of communication. By "communication" I mean one person talking to another person about some third reality. In order to interpret the social dimension of experience adequately, one needs to adopt a triadic rather than a di-polar construct.[21]

A triadic construct of experience discovers three irreducible variables in the higher forms of experience: evaluations, actions, and general tendencies.

Evaluations include the entire spectrum of human evaluative responses: sensations, feelings, images, hypotheses, deductive predictions, and inductive validations of deductively clarified hypotheses. Values yield a feeling of "particular suchness" since every evaluation has a particular character that distinguishes it from every other. Red is not green, is not angry, is not giraffe, is not right triangle.

Actions, by contrast, endow experience with concreteness. Choices make experience this rather than that. Actions, moreover, come in three generic forms: interactions, collaboration, and coercion. Actions forge social links.

Habitual tendencies, by contrast, endow experience with real generality and orient it to the future. They make experience tend to develop in one way rather than another. We grasp tendencies both inferentially and in judgments of feeling. In a triadic construct of experience, autonomously functioning tendencies count as selves, while selves capable of self-conscious responsibility count as persons.

Moreover, in a triadic construct of experience events signify. By that I mean that they have a dynamic relational structure that human evaluative responses can grasp; for actions express the laws, or tendencies, that give rise to them. When humans express symbolically to one another their evaluative responses to other persons or things, they communicate.[22]

These reflections highlight a serious contradiction in Schillebeeckx's understanding of experience. On the one hand, he postulates the social conditioning of experience. On the other hand, he opts for an epistemological construct of experience that lacks the categories to describe experience as social intercourse. Indeed, Schillebeeckx implicitly concedes the subjectivistic character of his di-polar construct when he asserts that linguistic and social conditioning enter experience from the "outside." In a triadic model, experience lacks such a clearly defined inside and outside, since what one experiences stands within experience and makes it into a certain kind of experience. Concrete actions create the social bonds linking autonomous experiences. Handing on traditions as well as imagining and creating a common future makes communities. Language and social conditioning also stand within experience; they do not enter it from the "outside." Indeed, language shapes intentionality.

Beyond any doubt, Schillebeeckx wants to develop a construct of experience that transcends Kantian solipsism; but he has failed to grasp that transcending Kantian solipsism requires a shift from a di-polar to a triadic construct of experience. The mere addition of external social conditioning to the subjective interrelation of percepts and concepts does not finally rescue a di-polar construct of experience from Kantian solipsism.

Schillebeeckx's subjectivistic construct of experience stands convicted of a second major philosophical blunder. By adopting an empiricist understanding of the perceptual pole of experience, Schillebeeckx espouses an indefensible conceptual nominalism. Had he studied C.S. Peirce's refutation of the nominalistic presuppositions of post-Cartesian, continental European philosophy, Schillebeeckx would have known better than to wander down this particular philosophical dead end. I shall examine Peirce's critique in some detail in the chapter that follows.

Here, however, we need to note that Peirce's realism differs from Platonic realism in its refusal to reify essences. Peirce correctly looked on essences, what he called "qualities," as particular, not general; as possible, not real. By generality, Peirce meant something closer to a subsisting, developing habit: namely, the real tendency inherent in things to act in predictable ways under specifiable conditions. Peirce argued correctly that the scientific mind grasps such tendencies inferentially as it articulates the developing laws that explain events.[23]

We also grasp real tendencies (and therefore real generality) in judgments of feeling. Fear, for example, tells me that, if I approach a coiled sidewinder too closely and that if I provoke it, it will tend to bite me, with injurious consequences to my body.[24]

Schillebeeckx, in opting for a di-polar construct of experience, reduces what we experience, the nature of the reality we encounter, to concrete percepts. Concrete percepts lack real generality. So do the concepts that the mind uses to interpret its percepts; for concepts, viewed in themselves and in abstraction from the way the mind uses them, display particularity, not real generality. Concepts do acquire logical generality through intentional use: namely, when we intend them to apply to all the individual members of a particular class; but concepts never lose their particularity. If **per absurdum** they did, they would lose their particular meaning and therefore their capacity to interpret. In and of themselves, however, concepts exemplify only particular possibilities.

Explanation grasps the significance of facts by grounding them in a law or real tendency. Nominalism, however, whether pure or conceptual, denies the reality of laws, of general tendencies. As a consequence, no nominalist can explain the significance of events. Instead, nominalism imposes meaning on surd and meaningless facts. In other words, Schillebeeckx's nominalistic, di-polar construct of experience lacks the categories it needs to explain why anything happens, including the act of interpretation.[25] I shall return to this last point in discussing the turn to experience in process theology.

The nominalism implicit in Schillebeeckx's construct of experience also makes it impossible to give an adequate account to human religious experience. Immanuel Kant saw most clearly the religious implications of the conceptual nominalism he defended. If concrete, sensible percepts exhaust knowable reality, then the idea of God must remain an empty concept.

Historically, the attempt to develop philosophically a theistic nominalism has led in two directions: either to idealism, as in the case of Berkeley and of Hegel, or to ontologism, as in the case of Whitehead and Malebranche. We need not look far to understand why. Nominalism equates reality with the concrete and the sensible. Unable to equate God with the concrete and sensible, theistic nominalists search for him in the conceptual pole of experience. They tend therefore to one of two fallacies: either they reduce the reality of the divine to a reified concept or they fallaciously defend the human mind's ability to grasp the divine ideas immediately. Schillebeeckx too searches for an experience of God in the conceptual pole of experience and claims to find it in a subjective, Spirit-inspired sense of having been saved.

Schillebeeckx seems finally to lapse into a kind of fideism. He clearly holds for the reality of God, but he proclaims the futility of trying to demonstrate the existence of God rationally and empirically. At the same time, his conceptual nominalism leaves him ill equipped to account for human religious experience. As we have seen, Schillebeeckx postulates a depth dimension to human experience which the action of the Holy Spirit discloses. If, however, divine revelation must transpire within the parameters of a di-polar human experience (as Schillebeeckx insists it must), then one may question with Kant whether the conditions for the possibility of such depth religious experiences actually exist. Schillebeeckx asserts that they do; but his nominalism deprives him of the conceptual tools he needs to explain how depth experiences happen. In the end, like Kant, he reduces the idea of God to an empty concept and appeals to apophatic mysticism to justify his position.

Here too, had Schillebeeckx pondered the advantages of a triadic construct of experience, he could have avoided all of these speculative impasses. As we have seen, only a triadic construct of experience can account for its social character. We enter into social relationships by interaction. When we interact socially, we grasp intuitively and inferentially the other selves with whom we interact. If God chooses to interact with a triadic human experience, then the human experience touched by God will perceive the divine reality as a transcendent, autonomous, personal tendency to act in specific ways, i.e. as a personal self. The Judeo-Christian tradition calls that autonomous divine self the Holy Spirit. Moreover, the free, historical self-disclosure of God in Jesus and in the Spirit creates a limited human capacity to predict how God will act. On the basis of Christian revelation, for example, one can assert confidently that God will do lovingly whatever God chooses to accomplish.

In the development of American religious philosophy, the mature Royce, rather than Peirce, articulated the speculative implications of a triadic construct of experience for Christian revelation. Royce did so in his monumental study: **The Problem of Christianity**. Royce saw that a triadic construct of experience makes the Spirit of God experienceable. He came to this conclusion, however, only after having reached what he called his "Peircean insight." By that he meant his shift from a di-polar construct of experience to Peirce's realistic, triadic construct. Peirce, moreover, explicitly approved Royce's explicitation of the theological implications of his position.[26]

Study of the classical American debate over the form and structure of experience could have helped Schillebeeckx avoid a fourth blunder. When Schillebeeckx talks about the interpretation of experience, he means either rational, inferential interpretation or supernatural faith. It does not seem to have occurred to him that the human mind, when left to its own resources, grasps reality in two different ways: imaginatively and intuitively, on the one hand, and rationally and inferentially, on the other. Again, had Schillebeeckx studied the classical American philosophers on experience he could have avoided this blunder. Classical American philosophy, in contrast to much continental European philosophy, traditionally and correctly defends the intuitive mind's capacity to grasp reality with judgments of feeling. Moreover, American philosophy correctly discovers strong analogies between religious and aesthetic experience.[27]

Schillebeeckx's failure to exploit these insights betrays him into implicitly equating interpretation with scientific, hypothetical-deductive thinking. Moreover, this assumption leaves him bereft of the hermeneutical tools he needs to interpret adequately the intuitive thought patterns of the New Testament writers. I find it striking, for example, that in the course of his three-volume study of the New Testament foundations for Christology, Schillebeeckx nowhere deals with narrative Christology as such. He makes his nearest approach in his handling of the Johannine tradition in his second volume.[28]

(III)

I have described Schillebeeckx's construct of experience and have argued that any attempt to explain experience as di-polar, as the subjective, rational interrelation of concrete percepts and particular concepts, falls into an indefensible conceptual nominalism and lacks the categories to account for human social and religious experience. In this final section of my argument, I shall attempt to show that Schillebeeckx's defense of a di-polar construct of experience fatally flaws his attempt to lay systematic New Testament foundations for Christology.

Schillebeeckx attempts to lay biblical foundations for Christology, but he does so as a systematic theologian. As a consequence, his flawed construct of experience provides his argument with its basic structure and most fundamental presuppositions. His first volume, **Jesus**, attempts to endow New Testament Christology with its perceptual content. To this end, it applies the methods of redaction criticism to summarize somewhat conservatively the results of the new quest for the historical Jesus. The second volume, **Christ**, attempts to provide New Testament Christology with its conceptual content by comparing and contrasting New Testament theologies of grace. The third volume, **Church**, summarizes the first two and appends miscellaneous reflections on the democratization of the Catholic Church.

Schillebeeckx knows perfectly well that his summary of the new quest for the historical Jesus yields, not raw perceptions of Jesus, but a theoretical reconstruction of what one can assert historically about Jesus with either certitude or high probability.[29] In the end, however, he believes that only the rational use of the methods of redaction criticism gives cognitive access to the facts about Jesus. Moreover, those facts mediate faith in the God that Jesus historically revealed. In other words, Schillebeeckx apparently expects the rational use of redaction criticism to supply faith with its "perceptual content."[30]

As long as Schillebeeckx deals with Jesus' mortal ministry, his method and epistemology serve him well enough. He offers an impressively documented summary of the bare historical facts about Jesus' public ministry, trial, and death. When he comes to speak about Jesus' resurrection, however, he reaches the limits of both his method and his epistemology.

Pheme Perkins and Reginald Fuller have summarized the chief exegetical problems with Schillebeeckx's handling of the resurrection. 1) They object that Schillebeeckx's attempt to ground the empty tomb tradition in an annual tomb cult has not a shred of hard evidence to ground it. 2) They argue that one cannot, as Schillebeeckx seems to assume, get behind the appearances of the risen Christ to some more primitive religious datum. The New Testament assertion "He appeared" provides Christian faith with its most primitive datum concerning the resurrection. 3) The New Testament witness belies Schillebeeckx's claim that the first Christians inferred the reality of the resurrection. Instead, the encounter with the risen Jesus bursts upon the disciples as something wholly unexpected, even incredible. 4) In deducing the reality of the resurrection from a subjective experience of conversion, Schillebeeckx confuses effect with cause. Those who saw the risen Christ did experience a conversion; but the encounter with the glorified Jesus precedes the conversion causally. Schillebeeckx's inferential interpretation of the resurrection, by contrast, makes resurrection faith fallaciously depend on conversion. The New Testament witness says the opposite, that conversion flowed from the encounter with the risen Christ. Had Schillebeeckx read the New Testament accurately in its witness to the resurrection, he would have opted for a Pauline appearance-mission model of the apostolic encounter with the risen Christ instead of the subjectivistic, conversion model he proposes. 5) Unlike the apostle Paul, Schillebeeckx fails to distinguish clearly between a resurrection encounter with the risen Christ and a vision of him.[31]

I agree with all of these objections and desire here only to call attention to the flawed epistemology that motivates this skewed reading of the New Testament witness to the resurrection. Schillebeeckx believes that revelation has to transpire within the parameters of experience as he has described it. He looks to the rational use of redaction criticism to provide faith with its perceptual pole by providing the empirical facts about Jesus. He realizes that by no stretch of the imagination can the resurrection qualify as a perceptual sense datum. Instead of recognizing the inadequacy of the empiricist presuppositions present in his construct, he concludes that, if resurrection faith has experiential grounding, it must find that grounding in the subjective, conceptual pole of experience. In other words, his inadequate construct of experience forces him to assert the inferential character of resurrection faith, even though the New Testament account of the origins of faith in the risen Christ says something very different.

Schillebeeckx's subjectivistic, di-polar construct of experience also forces him to ground belief in the reality of the resurrection in a subjective experience of conversion. Since, however, in his di-polar construct of experience, only empirical facts, or praxis, will endow experience with any objectivity, one finds oneself wondering whether an inference based on a subjective experience grasps something real or whether it imposes a meaning on empirical evidence that the evidence itself will not bear.

Once again a triadic construct of experience would keep one from such difficulties. In a triadic construct of experience events contain more than perceived, empirical facts. They also contain acting selves, acting persons. In a revelatory event, one experiences a divine person acting either directly or sacramentally. In other words, a triadic construct of experience finds no difficulty in talking about the resurrection as the experience of an encounter with a divine person mediated by that person's humanity totally transformed in God. In other words, a triadic construct of experience interprets both the social and religious experiences that Schillebeeckx's nominalistic, subjectivistic, di-polar construct cannot.

In my judgment, Schillebeeckx, having acquiesced in a vaguely Kantian construct of experience, in the end finds himself hoist on the same petard as Kant himself: namely, the mind's inability to know religious events as they are in themselves because faith, however derived, must impose on empirical facts an interpretation that those facts, as empirical, cannot themselves validate. I also believe that C.S. Peirce's systematic dismantling of Kantian epistemology has a lot to teach Schillebeeckx about the social and religious structure of experience. The next chapter examines Peirce's critique of Kant.

Schillebeeckx's decision to ground Christology in New Testament soteriology frustrates finally his attempt to lay biblical foundations for a systematic Christology in yet another way. Astonishingly enough, nowhere in his entire study does Schillebeeckx discuss New Testament Christology. His first volume discusses Jesusology, not Christology. His second volume discusses a New Testament theology of grace. The third volume summarizes the first two and appends miscellaneous, though often wise, reflections on contemporary ecclesiology.

Even if one concedes the legitimacy of the preceding criticisms of Schillebeeckx's work, his study will continue to rank as a major theological and scholarly achievement of the twentieth century. It provides a massively documented study of the new quest for the historical Jesus as well as a massively documented study of New Testament theologies of grace. Both volumes make solid contributions to New Testament theology, if not to New Testament Christology as such. In addition, all three volumes contain innumerable wise reflections on contemporary Christian experience.

Schillebeeckx has modestly called his study an "experiment in Christology," or better a prolegomenon to Christology.[32] His work exhibits impressive scholarly virtues, the fruit of a lifetime of patient theological reflection. When, however, one reflects on Schillebeeckx's work in the light of its fundamental goal—namely, laying New Testament foundations for a systematic Christology—I, for one, find myself ready to called his experiment a failed one.

The experiment has not failed for want of thorough scholarship. It fails because, somewhat in the manner of Anders Nygren's **Eros and Agape,** it provides massive scholarly documentation for a perverse hypothesis: in the case of Schillebeeckx, a fallacious, inadequate, nominalistic construct of experience that betrays an eminent scholar into avoiding the very topic he sought to investigate: namely, New Testament Christology.

Notes

[1]Edward Schillebeeckx, O.P., **Christ:The Experience of Jesus as Lord,** translated by John Bowen (New York: Seabury, 1980, p. 30.
[2]**Ibid.,** pp. 30-36.
[3]**Ibid.,** pp.134-43.
[4]**Ibid.,** pp. 36-40.
[5]Edward Schillebeeckx, O.P., **Church: The Human Story of God** (New York: Crossroad, 1990), pp. 46-49.
[6]**Ibid.,** pp. 15-22.
[7]**Ibid.,** pp. 27-28.
[8]**Ibid.,** pp. 46-53.
[9]**Ibid.,** pp.21-28.
[10]**Ibid.,** pp. 37-38.
[11]**Ibid.,** pp. 27-28.
[12]Schillebeeckx, **Jesus,** pp.43-48; **Church,** pp. 15-22; **Interim Report on the Books Jesus and Christ** (New York: Crossroad, 1981), pp. 10-19.
[13]Schillebeeckx, **Church,** pp. 23-28.
[14]Schillebeeckx, **Jesus,** pp. 34-40; **Church,** p. 211.
[15]Schillebeeckx, **Interim Report,** pp. 10-12.
[16]Schillebeeckx, **Church,** pp. 55-56, 66-68.
[17]**Ibid.,** pp. 73-76.
[18]**Ibid.,** pp. 77-78.
[19]Schillebeeckx, **Christ,** pp. 30-31.
[20]I include Dewey in this list with some hesitation, although his understanding of experience did distinguish habit from action and evaluation. His philosophy, however, focused more on the organic, environmentally conditioned character of experience than on its triadic structure. For Peirce and the mature Royce, however, the triadic structure of experience played a central role in their thought.

[21]Josiah Royce, **The Problem of Christianity** (2 vols.; Chicago: Regnery, 1968), vol. 2, pp. 109-63.

[22]For a further elaboration of this construct, see Donald L. Gelpi, S.J., **Grace as Transmuted Experience and Social Process: and Other Essays in North American Theology** (Lanham: University Press of America, 1988), pp.1-66.

[23]Peirce brought his mature thought on the triadic structure of experience to something like systematic statement in the lectures on pragmatism that he delivered in Sever Hall at Harvard University in 1903; cf. Charles Sanders Peirce, **Collected Papers**, edited by Charles Hartshorne and Paul Weiss (Cambridge: Harvard University Press, 1934), 5.14-212.

[24]Cf. Donald L. Gelpi, S.J., **Inculturating North American Theology: An Experiment in Foundational Method** (Atlanta: Scholars Press, 1988), pp.49-97.

[25]Cf. Donald L. Gelpi, S.J., **Experiencing God: A Theology of Human Emergence** (Lanham: University Press of America, 1987), pp. 65-75.

[26]By the time Royce wrote **The Problem of Christianity**, his notion of Spirit had become less philosophical and more theological, less Hegelian and more Pauline. For a superb study of the mature Royce on religious experience, see Frank M. Oppenheim, S.J., **Royce's Mature Philosophy of Religion** (Notre Dame: Notre Dame University Press, 1987).

[27]Cf. Gelpi, **Grace as Transmuted Experience and Social Process**, pp. 11-22. Hans Urs Von Balthasar provides an interesting example of a European theologian very much attuned to the aesthetic dimensions of faith. Cf. Hans Urs Von Balthasar, **Love Alone: The Way of Revelation** (London: Burns and Oates, 1968); **The Glory of the Lord: A Theological Aesthetics**, translated by Erasmo Leiva-Mankakis (5 vols.; New York: Crossroad, 1983 ff).

[28]Schillebeeckx, **Christ**, pp. 305-462; cf. Gelpi, **Inculturating North American Theology**, pp. 49-97. Even in dealing with the gospel of John, Schillebeeckx fails to read the gospel as narrative theology but attempts instead to distill from it its overall cosmic vision.

[29]Schillebeeckx, **Interim Report**, pp. 20-35.

[30]**Ibid.,** pp. 10-16, 27-35.

[31]Reginald H. Fuller and Pheme Perkins, **Who Is This Christ? Gospel Christianity and Contemporary Faith** (Philadelphia: Fortress, 1983), pp.28-37.

[32]Schillebeeckx, **Jesus**, pp. 35-36.

2

Praxis and the Turn to
Experience in Liberation Theology

Liberation theology makes the turn to experience when it places praxis at the heart of theological thinking. The term "praxis" has many meanings in liberation theology. Often the same author will use it in more than one sense. The term, however, tends to connote coordinated, practical action to rectify unjust and oppressive social structures.

The turn to praxis implies the turn to experience because theologians of praxis attempt to read divine revelation through the eyes of the poor and the oppressed. In other words, the experience of oppression provides the lens that brings the meaning of Christian revelation into focus.

As liberation theology has evolved, some liberation theologians have recognized the need to clarify the meaning of praxis. Moreover, as we shall see, some have tended to define "praxis" in much the same way that Schillebeeckx defines "experience." The debate within Latin American liberation theology about the relationship between orthodoxy and orthopraxis illustrates the speculative tendencies to which I refer.

In the preface to the fifteenth anniversary edition of **The Theology of Liberation** Gustavo Gutierrez, the founder of Latin American liberation theology, has reflected with his customary insight and sensitivity on the developments in liberation theology that have transpired since the first publication of that seminal work. In the course of his reflections, he calls, among other things, for more systematic theological reflection on the relationship between orthodoxy and orthopraxis.[1] This chapter attempts to respond to that call by drawing on the insights of two giants of the

North American philosophical tradition, C.S. Peirce, the founder of philosophical pragmatism, and John Dewey, who developed pragmatic thinking in an instrumentalist direction.

In **The American Evasion of Philosophy: A Genealogy of Pragmatism,** Cornel West has discovered prophetic potential in the American pragmatic tradition.[2] I agree on the whole with his argument and also offer the following reflections in support of his thesis. Latin American liberation theologians have learned from black liberation theologians like West to acknowledge the role that racism plays in third world oppression. I would hope that, through a study of West's work, they might also begin to take the North American pragmatists as philosophical interlocutors.

As I believe this chapter will show, the pragmatists can indeed advance the prophetic agenda of Latin American liberationists. Moreover, as I shall also show, their systematic repudiation of the Cartesian and Kantian "turn to the subject" makes them far more fruitful philosophical interlocutors than either transcendental Thomism or Immanuel Kant in liberation theology's ongoing search to justify its theological turn to politics, economics, and the search for a just social order.

My argument divides into four parts. In the first, I shall attempt to argue in favor of Gutierrez's suggestion that liberation theology has yet to offer an adequate account of the relationship between orthodoxy and orthopraxis. I shall do so principally by examining the work of two liberation theologians who have addressed this question somewhat systematically: Juan Luis Segundo and Clodovis Boff. I shall argue then that the pragmatism of C.S. Peirce and the instrumentalism of John Dewey offer important insights into three interrelated issues that yield a sound grasp of the fundamental relationship between orthodoxy and orthopraxis. I am referring to the following issues: 1) the dynamic relationship between thought and action in reality and in thought; 2) the instrumental character of all shared inquiry, including shared theological inquiry; and 3) the relationship between strictly normative thinking and orthodoxy. The second, third, and fourth sections of my argument will examine each of these issues in turn.

(I)

Within liberation theology the contrast between orthodoxy and orthopraxis arises from a common criticism voiced by liberation theologians. They fault classical, apolitical, academic forms of theology as well as much of the church's official pastoral magesterium for too much concern with orthodoxy, or doctrinal truth, and not enough concern with orthopraxis, or obedience to the moral demands of the gospel, especially in the area of public morality.

Just how orthodoxy and orthopraxis relate remains somewhat vague in Gutierrez's own thought, as his call for the clarification of this issue suggests. Gutierrez defines the term "praxis" as liberating social action informed by a Christian spirituality and therefore by Christian love.[3] Within the arena of praxis he envisages the dynamic interplay of theory and practice; but he describes theology as critical reflection on praxis.[4] His profound respect for the autonomy of the poor in the advancement of a liberating praxis leaves Gutierrez unwilling as a theologian to set the social, economic, and political agenda **for** the poor. That the poor must do for themselves.[5] As a consequence, he distances theological reflection from the dynamic interplay of thought and action within praxis. Theology reflects critically on the praxis of the poor but one level of abstraction removed from praxis itself.

In other words, within the praxis situation, Gutierrez seems to espouse something like a vigorous instrumentalism; but, when he describes the work of theology, which advances at a second level of abstraction from praxis, he describes its method as critical reflection upon praxis. Gutierrez has not reflected systematically on theological method. His language leaves one suspecting, however, that while the autonomous poor guide praxis instrumentally, theology advances through the implementation within faith of something akin to a Kantian critical logic. Gutierrez's endorsement of a Marechalian anthropology reinforces this suspicion; for Marechal and those theologians he has inspired have attempted to update Thomistic anthropology by using Kantian critical method.[6] Kantian logic, unfortunately, sunders speculative from practical reason in a way that leaves one wondering how ever to reunite them.

In calling for more reflection on the relationship between orthodoxy and orthopraxis, Gutierrez is also implicitly professing his dissatisfaction with the attempts of other liberation theologians to deal with this question. Among Latin American liberation theologians, two have treated the issue with some thoroughness: Juan Luis Segundo in **The Liberation of Theology** and in **Faith and Ideologies** and Clodovis Boff in **Theology and Praxis.**

In **The Liberation of Theology** Segundo challenged academic theologians to complete the hermeneutic circle by beginning their thinking with the social analysis of human oppression, then advancing to critical theological reflection on the analyzed situation in the light of the gospel, and finally returning to the situation with faith-derived formulas for overcoming injustice.[7]

In **The Liberation of Theology**, however, Segundo's discussion of the relationship between faith and ideology leaves one bereft of faith-derived norms for choosing one's political and economic path. Faith, Segundo argues, orients us to the Absolute. Ideology deals with the practicalities of social transformation. Segundo defines ideology in this early work as "some idea . . . of the goal of the revolutionary process and the proper means to be used to achieve it." Since, however, the Absolute utterly transcends history, not only does faith in the Absolute lack specific cognitive content, but it provides no norms whatsoever for choosing among ideologies.[8] (One suspects that Rahner's theology of God as absolute mystery lies behind Segundo's conception of God as Absolute.)

In other words, while Segundo in **The Liberation of Theology** insists that theology must complete the hermeneutic circle, he seems to define faith in such a way as to make that task impossible.[9]

In **Faith and Ideologies**, the situation has not improved significantly. In this later study, Segundo now defines "faith" as an ordering consent to the realm of value which necessarily subordinates every other value to an absolute value.[10] He also broadens his definition of "ideology" to include all human knowledge about efficacy.[11] In my opinion, not only does the later Segundo fail to provide a convincing argument that the human attempt to order values forces consent to the Absolute, but he also arbitrarily defines the realm of efficacy as devoid of value. He also assigns to scientific thinking rather than to theology the systematic theoretical exploration of this valueless realm.[12]

In other words, by dualistically separating value from action and theory from practice, Segundo seems as far in **Faith and Ideologies** from closing the hermeneutic circle in principle as he was in **The Liberation of Theology**.

Clodovis Boff in **Theology and Praxis** offers a clearer as well as a subtler interpretation of the relationship between religious belief and political practice than Segundo's. Boff argues that the social analysis of unjust situations provides political theology with its material object.[13] By "praxis" **Boff** means "the **complexus of practices** orientated (sic) to the transformation of society, the making of history."[14] By the end of his analysis, however, Boff has transformed the term "praxis" into a quasi-metaphysical term. He equates "praxis" with being, the concrete, facts, experience, history, life, the material.[15] Theory functions within praxis through the instrumentality of "theoretical praxis," or method. Theology exemplifies one kind of purely theoretical, speculative thinking.

Among its many merits, Boff's study correctly argues that the question of the relationship of theology to praxis in the last analysis raises epistemological issues. As we have seen, one finds hints of Kantianism in the thought of both Gutierrez and Segundo in their apparent endorsement of Marechalian or Rahnerian anthropology. Kantianism surfaces even more explicitly in Boff's analysis. With Kant he argues that because human reason, including theological reason, constructs its object, the human mind has no access to the thing in itself.[16] Moreover, with Kant (and Schillebeeckx) he defends a species of percept-concept epistemology. Praxis, broadly defined as being, the concrete, facts, experience, history, life, the material functions in his epistemology more or less as the sense manifold does in Kant's. Praxis provides the raw materials of thought. Theory, whether scientific or theological, provides the concepts that transform the matter of praxis into intelligible objects of thought.[17]

Moreover, Boff shows much concern to vindicate the purely

theoretical character of theological reasoning. While he insists on the importance of political theology, he shows considerable concern to inoculate speculative theology against a political virus. Boff does not want theologians meddling directly in political praxis, nor does he want politics to dictate speculative conclusions to the theologian. As a consequence, Boff argues that theology has only an extrinsic relationship to secular political practice. By that he means that the person who engages in abstract theological thinking according to the autonomous principles of theological method also happens to have specific political commitments. Similarly, the conclusions drawn by theologians on purely theoretical, apolitical grounds may by chance have some extrinsic relationship to the practical, political order; but theology has no direct or immediate relationship to the political. When theology has influence on the political, something non-theological needs to mediate that influence: either scientific, social analysis of the political situation or concrete Christian political praxis.[18] Moreover, Boff settles for a purely extrinsic, mediated relationship between theological thinking and political praxis because, like Kant, he finds an unbridgeable gulf, a **chorsimos**, between theory and practice.[19]

Clearly, Gutierrez does well to call for further theological reflection on the relationship between orthodoxy and orthopraxis, between Christian belief and liberating political praxis. He himself has not dealt systematically with this issue, while both Segundo and Boff leave as wide a gulf between theoretical and practical reason as did Immanuel Kant, whose flawed logic and epistemology have so mightily influenced so much continental European theology. Moreover, it would seem that through their formative exposure to European theological thinking, more than one Latin liberation theologian has caught the Kantian virus.

(II)

In this second section of my argument, I will try to show that the pragmatism of C.S. Peirce casts important light on the relationship between thought and action in reality and in the human grasp of the real.

In his seminal study of the relationship between thought and action, **Praxis and Action**, Richard Bernstein correctly notes that the continental European mind has on the whole failed to understand and even less to appreciate the pragmatic philosophies of Peirce and Dewey.[20] Moreover, as I have pondered the achievement of both of these men, I have reached the conviction that they would provide liberation theology with fruitful interlocutors whose insights would enhance the work of liberation theology itself. More specifically, I believe that Peirce's pragmatism holds the speculative key that unlocks the puzzling problem of the relationship between rational belief and action. In illuminating this philosophical issue Peirce's pragmatism also points toward a sound understanding of the relationship between orthodoxy and orthopraxis.

Moreover, Peirce, I believe, can help liberation theologians (and, as we shall see, Catholic transcendental theologians as well) move beyond the hopeless inadequacies of Kantian logic and epistemology. Peirce began his religious and philosophical career as a vague New England transcendentalist.[21] American transcendentalists like Ralph Waldo Emerson and Theodore Parker acknowledged a speculative debt to Kant; but Peirce did something that neither of these two reverend gentlemen ever did. For three years Peirce actually read **The Critique of Pure Reason** every day for several hours until, by his own testimony, he could recite long passages by heart.[22] He stopped the practice when he saw through Kantian logic.

Peirce mounted a devastating criticism of Kantian logic and epistemology. As a consequence of his own detailed studies of medieval and of modern logic, Peirce had concluded that the rational mind employs three distinct and irreducible forms of inference whenever it reasons: abductive, or hypothetical, reasoning; deductive, or predictive, reasoning; and inductive, or validating, reasoning.[23] Moreover, the mature Peirce saw that the same forms of inference that structure reasoning on secular matters also give logical structure to religious reasoning as well; for the same human mind that reasons about secular problems reasons about religious questions as well. Whatever the context, that mind must make do with the same forms of rational inference because it has no other forms of rational thinking to employ.[24]

Peirce correctly criticized Kant for his failure to distinguish clearly these three forms of reasoning. As a result of that failure, Kant's transcendental method formulates an unverified hypothesis about how the human mind works and then presents it as an induction, as a validated hypothesis, while calling it a transcendental deduction. In fact, Peirce argued, Kant's epistemology offers not only an unvalidated hypothesis about the way the mind works but a demonstrably false hypothesis to boot.[25]

Peirce found three irreducible elements in abduction, deduction, and induction. He described these three logical elements as a rule, a case, and a result. A rule enunciates a general principle of reason. A result designates a concrete event or series of events in need of rational explanation. A case furnishes the categories we use in explaining results rationally.

Moreover, the three forms of inference—abduction, deduction, and induction—differ irreducibly from one another because each kind of inference interrelates rule, case, and result differently. An abduction, or hypothetical inference, concludes to a case. On the basis of a rule that it assumes to hold in reality, it uses the conceptions of the mind to categorize puzzling facts that need an explanation.[26]

For example, as the young Columbus seated at oceanside watched ships approach on a clear day, he noticed that first the tips of the masts, then the masts, then the hull came into view. Columbus then reasoned that if the ship sailed on a flat surface that would not occur: we would see the whole ship tiny in the distance but becoming larger and larger as it approached. If, however, the ship sailed on a curved sea, it would appear to the eye exactly as it did to his. Columbus therefore argued that the forces of nature must have made the world round, not flat. In recategorizing the world as round, Columbus sought to explain the fact of how the approaching ship appeared to him. Columbus made his abduction on the basis of a principle that he assumed to operate in nature: namely, that the forces of nature had conspired to make the world round, not flat.

Having inferred abductively the roundness of the earth,

Columbus then engaged in a deductive, or predictive inference. Deductive inference argues that, if a given hypothesis has interpreted reality correctly, then new facts, facts different from the facts that originally motivated the hypothesis, will under specifiable circumstances make their appearance. Columbus, for example, reasoned deductively that, if he had correctly categorized the earth as round, then he could reach the Orient by sailing west instead of east. In other words, while abductive inference concludes to a case, deductive inference concludes to facts implied by an abduction but not yet in evidence.

Eventually, Magellan's crew provided the data necessary to validate Columbus's initial hypothesis when they circumnavigated the globe. Their achievement provided the facts needed to conclude decisively that, when Columbus enunciated the principle that the forces of nature had made the world round rather than flat, he had grasped the truth about the way nature shaped the world. Drawing that conclusion exemplifies inductive inference.

Hence, abductive inference concludes to a case, to a new categorization of reality. Deductive inference concludes to a result by predicting on the basis of an hypothesis that new facts will turn up under specifiable conditions if the hypothesis holds true. Inductive, or validating, inference concludes to a rule by arguing that the appearance of the predicted facts gives evidence that the laws, or generalized tendencies, that the abductive mind had assumed to shape events actually do so. Inductive inference invalidates an hypothesis when the predicted facts fail to materialize; or it can validate an hypothesis only within a range of probability.

Peirce's account of the three forms of inference holds the key to understanding the meaning of his pragmatic maxim; moreover, the pragmatic maxim throws critical light on the relationship between rational thought and action and implicitly on the relationship between orthodoxy and orthopraxis. Peirce first formulated the pragmatic maxim in the following terms: "Consider what effects, that might conceivably have practical bearings, we conceive the object of our conception to have. Then, our conception of these effects is the whole of our conception of the object."[27] Read in the light of Peirce's theory of inference, the pragmatic maxim is asserting: if you want to think clearly and rationally about something, then formulate a hypothesis about it and deduce its operational consequences. Those operational consequences, correctly deduced, articulate the rational meaning of the hypothesis you have formulated.

Peirce saw correctly that, if he had understood correctly the way that human reason functions, then rational thinking cannot advance except through the dynamic interplay of thought and action within the process of inquiry itself. We cannot understand the nature of the world through some Cartesian meditation on the nature of reality. We can grasp the world only by interacting with it. Action, choice, decision contribute something indispensable to the mind's conquest of truth. We must interact with the realities we think about in order to create the experimental situations that will validate or invalidate our hypotheses about them. Columbus had only one way to test his hypothesis. He had to try to sail around the world.

Even more, action enters into our very grasp of the constitutive nature of things. We understand the real nature of a thing when we grasp the laws, the generalized tendencies, that ground its behavior; for only a sound understanding of those laws allows us to predict how a thing will act and the circumstances under which it will do so.

Finally, in formulating the pragmatic maxim, Peirce saw correctly that the validation of a hypothesis never happens at a purely theoretical level. Validation demands belief; and belief demands the commitment to take responsibility for the consequences of the propositions one asserts. One takes responsibility for a proposition by standing by it until one finds a good reason to call it into question. One can identify three good reasons for calling a belief into question: 1) a fact that contradicts the belief, 2) a contradiction between one's belief and other beliefs one professes to hold, or 3) consequences flowing from one's belief that jeopardize one's own good or that of others.

Peirce had pondered deeply the medieval debates between nominalists and realists. He deemed himself particularly indebted to the thought of John Duns Scotus.[28] Peirce sided with the realists against the nominalists; but his logical studies had taught him not to reify essences in the manner of classical Platonism and Aristotelianism. We need, he insisted, to assert the presence of real generality in things; but the real generality in things consists of the laws that cause activity, laws that in protoplasm and in the higher forms of life exhibit an extraordinary plasticity and developmental complexity.[29]

These insights allowed Peirce to mount a second devastating critique of Kant's epistemology. Kantian theory of knowledge peddled philosophical nominalism.[30] Kant's real universe contained only concrete, individual facts. It lacked any real generality because, for Kant, the mind imposes universality subjectively upon concrete sense data. It does not grasp the real generality in things. Indeed, in Kant, the mind can never know the thing-in-itself. Instead of having grasped the conditions for the possibility of scientific thinking, Kant denied the two conditions that make scientific thinking possible, the real existence of law, of conditioned generality, in the very constitution of things and the mind's ability to grasp those laws inferentially.

Peirce found yet another fatal flaw in Kantian logic and theory of knowledge. Not only did Kant fail to distinguish clearly the three fundamental forms of inference and in the process lapse into an indefensible nominalism; but he also proposed an individualistic understanding of human reason that has little relationship to the way the human mind actually works. Of the three forms of inference, only deductive inference can claim logical necessity. The mind needs to formulate its hypotheses before it knows whether it has amassed all the data relevant to the resolution of any complex problem. Moreover, even if one validates an hypothesis, one does so within a particular frame of reference. Given the finitude of human reason, one has no assurance that some other mind might not conceive a more adequate frame of reference than the frame of reference one espouses and so force one to revise one's conclusions. Nor can the temporary validation of a hypothesis prevent some other investigator from turning up facts that call one's original conclusions into question. In other words, at the two critical points in reasoning at which the mind touches reality, it finds itself forced to employ radically fallible forms of argumentation.

For Peirce, this fallibilistic interpretation of the human mind offered hope not discouragement. It means, he argued, that one has a much better chance of grasping the nature of things if one recognizes that one can make a mistake than if one refuses to acknowledge that possibility. The confession of fallibility also forces anyone committed to discovering the truth to recognize the social, dialogic character of all systematic inquiry. Fallible minds need to profit from the experience and insight of other minds if they hope to understand themselves and their world. Instead of consisting in a solipsistic Cartesian (or Kantian) meditation, rational thinking consists in ongoing social dialogue. If we hope to understand the truth, we need to commit ourselves to a community of truth seekers and by learning from one another's experience and insight advance toward the best explanation of events that we can formulate.[31]

Moreover, pragmatic logic has a self-corrective principle built into it. If we make false assumptions about reality, reality itself will tell us so by refusing to behave in the ways in which our hypotheses predict it will. When that happens we know we need to take our abductions back to the drawing board. In other words, if we take the pragmatic maxim seriously, if we commit ourselves to thinking clearly about reality, if we therefore clarify deductively the operational consequences of our hypotheses and then validate them or invalidate them inductively, then the world will gradually teach us which laws govern its behavior and which do not.

Peirce recognized that one could use his pragmatic logic of consequences to build bridges and dams or even to rectify unjust social situations. He found himself, however, fascinated by the speculative, metaphysical implications of his insights into logic and epistemology. Reality, he saw, had to have an irreducibly triadic structure. Acting selves embody the laws, the dynamic tendencies that orient the world toward a specific kind of future. Facts, concrete actions endow the universe with its developing social structure. Finally, qualities, evaluative responses to dynamically acting selves, make us present to our world and it to us.[32]

The symbolic nature of the human mind also makes it consciously social. The symbolic nature of the mind makes it possible for individuals to join communities of shared systematic inquiry, communities committed to uncovering the truth of things through collaborative investigation. Having reached these conclusions, Peirce saw that they force yet another important critique of Kant. Kant had fallaciously assumed that thinking consists only in interrelating concrete percepts with abstract and universal concepts. On such an hypothesis, all thinking takes place between one's ears. As a consequence, a Kantian theory of knowledge has no way to explain the fundamental human experience of conversation, of one person talking to another about some third reality. Only a triadic construct of experience can account for the irreducibly social and symbolic character of human life and thus disclose what Peirce called "Man's Glassy Essence."[33]

Among the liberation theologians who have struggled with the relationship of orthodoxy to orthopraxis, Clodovis Boff has perhaps grasped most clearly that a sound understanding of that relationship raises questions that only epistemology can answer. Unfortunately, however, he seems to assume the adequacy of Kantian logic and epistemology to provide the answer. I find Peirce's critique of Kant a devastating refutation of that assumption.

Moreover, were liberation theology to adopt a Peircean rather than a Kantian epistemology and logic as the basis for rational theological thinking, it would, I believe, begin to lay sound epistemological foundations for understanding the intimate relationship between orthodoxy and orthopraxis.

Peircean pragmatism calls us beyond the essence fallacy, beyond the classical reification of essences that has confused the theological mind by convincing it that the intellect alone can plunge through metaphysical insight to the essential nature of things. By the principles of Peircean logic we understand any reality rationally, including the reality of God, by understanding how God deals with us habitually and under what circumstances. We understand who Jesus Christ is by understanding how he relates to us habitually and under what circumstances. We understand the doctrine of the Trinity and of the incarnation clearly only when we grasp the practical consequences of assent to it. Indeed, until we grasp those practical consequences, our theoretical explanations of such doctrines wallow in rational vagueness. Moreover, we will understand reality, including the reality of divine things, only by interacting with the very realities we are trying to understand.

Were Boff to shift from a vaguely Kantian logic and epistemology to a Peircean one, he would, I believe, have to call into question the purely theoretical nature of theological thinking and would possess the philosophical tools he needs to pursue the kind of political theology that he passionately espouses. Peirce's logic and epistemology could, I believe, also help Gutierrez (and probably Segundo) recognize the methodological fallacies that lie at the basis of Marechalian and Rahnerian anthropology.[34]

Peirce's logic and theory of knowledge could also help liberation theologians recognize that theology involves much more than Kantian critical reflection on the dynamic interplay of theory and practice. That interplay lies at the very heart of the theological enterprise itself. To this question we turn in the section that follows.

(III)

I have suggested that classical American pragmatism raises three issues that help throw light on the relationship of orthodoxy and orthopraxis. In the preceding section of this article, I have examined the first of these two issues: the dynamic interplay of thought and action in the rational appropriation of reality. I have argued that a sound insight into inferential thinking puts action at the heart of theoretical understanding. It does so for three reasons: 1) We do not grasp rationally what any reality is until we have grasped the laws, the general tendencies that make it act in predictable ways. 2) We cannot either verify or falsify our hypothetical interpretations of reality without interacting with the realities we are trying to interpret. 3) We never fix our beliefs in a purely theoretical way because the fixation of every belief demands a practical commitment to stand by its consequences until we have a good reason to call that belief into question.

In the present section, I shall reflect on the second issue that classical American pragmatism raises that throws light on the relationship between orthodoxy and orthopraxis: namely, the instrumental character of all shared systematic inquiry, including shared, systematic, theological inquiry. Among the American pragmatists, John Dewey developed in greatest detail the notion of instrumentalism. His insights, however, build on the speculative foundations that Peirce had laid.

Peirce recognized that one could use pragmatic logic to do practical things like building bridges or transforming the world; but he found himself more intrigued by the speculative and metaphysical implications of pragmatic logic than by its instrumental use. While Peirce's pragmatism derived from a critical repudiation of Kantian logic and epistemology, Dewey's pragmatic instrumentalism resulted from his critique of Hegelian idealism. Dewey set himself the task of naturalizing Hegel. He went about that task by grounding human experience and understanding, not in the dialectics of Spirit, but in the embodied, organic character of human life and experience.

Dewey held that biology prepares and foreshadows the social dynamics of inquiry. All organic life, including human life, develops in dynamic interaction with its environment. An organism in tune with its environment finds itself in a state of life-giving equilibrium. An organism experiences need as the disturbance of that equilibrium.[35]

Shared human inquiry responds to human needs because it arises from the conscious disturbance of environmental equilibrium. Inquiry always occurs in a culturally conditioned environment. In the case of human experience, cultural heredity modifies organic behavior with linguistic and symbolic insight. Language shapes and transmits institutional modes of perception and behavior, permeates the forms and contents of all other cultural activities, and endows them with a distinctive dynamic structure and form. Events signify, but linguistically conditioned symbols endow events with meaning, thus giving events their capacity to signify something to someone.[36]

When humans think, they interact with their culturally conditioned environments. They think in situations, about the situations in which they find themselves, and about themselves in those situations. The situations that engage human thought constitute a contextual whole. Moreover, conscious, focused thought advances against the background of a felt, qualitative sense of that contextual unity.[37]

Dewey believed that shared systematic inquiry responds to significant states of disequilibrium in the human environment. He therefore defined inquiry as "the controlled or directed transformation of an indeterminate situation into one that is so determinate in its constituent distinctions and relations as to convert the elements of the original situation into a unified whole."[38]

Situations become indeterminate with respect to an issue. Inquiry into the situation must begin, therefore, by identifying the locus of the problem it needs to solve. No human situation suffers from total indeterminacy. A totally indeterminate situation would correspond to absolute chaos and defy any kind of creative resolution. Isolating the problem in a situation partially out of control begins to resolve its indeterminacy. Ordinarily one identifies the nature of the problem progressively. As one clarifies the nature of the problem confronting one, possible solutions begin to suggest themselves.[39]

All inquiry seeks to come to a settled judgment about an indeterminate situation. A settled judgment brings the situation to a satisfactory resolution. As the inquiry proceeds, it seeks to reconstruct the situation. Theories, therefore, function instrumentally within situations. They seek to derive from knowledge of what is settled in a situation of disequilibrium the means of reducing that situation to a state of life-giving equilibrium. Affirmation and negation function in the instrumental resolution of a problematic situation.[40]

One resolves a problematic situation by transforming it into one that yields shared consummatory experiences. Consummatory experiences enhance and fulfill the human. The shared character of human life and inquiry also requires the shared character of human consummations.[41]

As Lonergan's reflections on method in theology make clear, theology qualifies as shared systematic inquiry. As shared inquiry theology faces two fundamental tasks: the retrieval of the Christian tradition and its critical, inculturated reformulation.[42]

Both tasks result from situations of disequilibrium in the Christian community. Disequilibrium in the retrieval of the Christian tradition derives from two sources: scholarly investigations that call into question contemporary assumptions about how the Christian tradition evolved and the need to communicate the knowledge of that tradition to each new generation of Christians.

Local churches of necessity understand church history from a limited cultural perspective. The systematic scholarly retrieval of the past tends as a consequence to pose regular challenges to the cultural assumptions that any group of contemporary Christians brings to the understanding of Christian origins. The ego inertia present in common sense thinking betrays people all too easily into assuming that the church always had the familiar shape it now possesses. A careful study of Christian origins, however, quickly belies that assumption. Among contemporary theologians Edward Schillebeeckx excels in his ability to use the pluralism of history in order to relativize contemporary assumptions about the presuppositions, organization, and beliefs of the Christian community.

Whenever breakthroughs in scholarly research demand the revision of our understanding of the historical origins of the Christian community, those breakthroughs create the practical need for the church to reach a new consensus concerning its foundation and historical evolution. Why? Because such consensus creates the church's shared faith consciousness and because shared faith consciousness creates in turn the Christian community's present sense of shared identity. In other words, the ongoing retrieval of Christian origins serves a very real instrumental need within the church: the achievement of an ongoing consensus about the historical identity of the Christian community. As the Protestant reformation dramatizes, when consensus about the meaning of Christian origins shatters, so does the church. Moreover, without that consensus the church finds itself bereft of the sense of shared identity it needs in order to reach a consensus about the corporate future to which God calls it. Once again, the failure of the Christian churches in the wake of the Protestant reformation to reach a consensus on church order and discipline dramatizes the problem of which I speak.

Besides reaching scholarly consensus about its origins, the church faces another perennial challenge that creates within it a situation of ongoing theological disequilibrium. I am speaking of the need to communicate to each new generation of Christians a sound understanding of Christian origins. That communication needs to happen in a variety of cultural contexts that pose different catechetical challenges to Christian teachers.

An instrumental approach to theological thinking attuned to the demands of inculturated evangelization demands that, in advancing the work of evangelization, theology contributes actively to the resolution of religious situations marred by pathology, immorality, lies, oppression, injustice, and religious unbelief. In accomplishing that task, theology has to employ an instrumental logic that devises strategies for calling both communities and individuals to integral conversion before God.

In my own judgment, the recent pastoral letters of the North American bishops on peace and economic justice illustrate admirably how theology can think instrumentally within a problematic religious situation. The process the bishops used in writing these pastorals also showed that they understand the basics of instrumental logic. The bishops began by identifying two situations that pose a direct challenge to the Christian conscience: the escalating arms race and the injustices born of trickle-down economics. They held systematic public hearings in order to clarify the nature of these two problems and in order to identify the stable resources present in Christian faith that might contribute to their resolution. The bishops tried to provide a forum for every viewpoint that might have something to contribute to naming the problems accurately and to resolving them. Public debate of the various drafts of each pastoral also invited widespread input from as broad a spectrum of respondents as possible.

The argument of the pastorals also illustrates well how instrumental logic functions in theological thinking. After an analysis of the problem in hand, both pastorals summarize the gospel truths and values relevant to the problem each addresses. The pastorals then derive from the gospel principles that point the way toward a practical resolution of the problematic situation that concerns them. From those principles, the pastorals then derive practical policies that promise to transform the situation. Finally, the pastorals urge the creation of concrete strategies for implementing those policies.

I doubt that the American bishops or those who advised them drew consciously on Dewey's philosophy in writing these two pastorals. Nevertheless, both the process of writing and documents written illustrate admirably the methods of instrumental thinking that Dewey describes.

I have been arguing that the pragmatic logics of Dewey and Peirce offer theology a valid speculative alternative to the flawed logic and epistemology of Immanuel Kant that tantalizes so many contemporary Catholic theologians. By recognizing both the dynamic interplay of thought and action within all human thinking, including theological thinking, pragmatic logic undercuts the artificial sundering of theory from practice that Kant helped popularize. It suggests that instead of portraying theology as a purely theoretical enterprise in the manner of Clodovis Boff, all theologians, including liberation theologians, need to recognize the instrumental, situational character of theological thinking.

I would also argue that pragmatic logic offers important insights into how one goes about deriving the norms for rendering indeterminate religious situations determinate. In order to resolve that question, however, we need to examine the third insight that pragmatic logic brings to a sound understanding of the relationship between orthodoxy and orthopraxis. I am referring to Peirce's account of the relationship between what he calls normative thinking and the grasp of reality. To these issues we turn in the fourth and final section of this chapter.

(IV)

Peirce understood his pragmatic maxim as a principle of explanatory logic. He invoked it within the logic of abduction in order to test the clarity and therefore the testability of particular hypotheses. As we saw in part two of this article, pragmatic logic argues that one grasps clearly what a thing is, its essence, when one can predict how it will act and under what conditions. Any hypothesis that cannot make such a prediction qualifies as vague and therefore untestable.

As we also saw, pragmatic logic demands that we must interact with the realities we are trying to understand if we hope to validate or invalidate our hypotheses about them. If we do, then the realities we are trying to understand will gradually disclose their nature to us by the way they behave.

As a principle of explanatory logic, the pragmatic maxim blurs somewhat the traditional distinction between "is" propositions and "ought" propositions; for in pragmatic logic one understands what a thing is when one grasps the law that allows one to predict how it ought to behave under specifiable circumstances. Pragmatic logic also blurs the distinction between speculative and evaluative thinking. All thinking involves evaluation, for only through evaluation does the human mind become present to the realities it is trying to understand.[43]

Nevertheless, Peirce also made a place within philosophical thinking for what he called "normative thinking." Moreover, he found in normative thinking a different kind of normativity from that manifested in rational explanation. In normative thinking one measures one's own conduct in the light of ideals, values, and principles that one has come to recognize as personally binding. Peirce discovered such normative thinking in three philosophical sciences: aesthetics, ethics, and logic.

For a long time, Peirce felt loathe to include aesthetics among the normative sciences on the principle that one should never argue about matters of taste (**de gustibus non est disputandum**). He changed his mind, however, when he realized that one can study in a systematic way the practical, self-critical cultivation of the kind of healthy affectivity that responds to beauty. The normative science of aesthetics yields, therefore, an insight into how to cultivate the affective and imaginative habits that allow one to appreciate genuine excellence. It identifies the ideals, realities, and values that make life worth living and teaches one how to perceive those realities imaginatively and affectively.[44]

Among the beautiful realities that endow life with purpose, meaning, and value, Peirce included the reality of God.[45] Kantian nominalists correctly argue that, on nominalist principles, one can never experience God as an object of knowledge. In the world of Kantian nominalism, only sensory experience provides the raw material of real knowing, and God cannot be reduced to an object of sense. Peirce's pragmatic realism, however, undercuts the claims of both Kantian nominalism and the British empiricism that inspired it by arguing that we experience, not just factual interactions but real generality, the dynamic tendencies that ground and explain concrete actions. We experience real generality inferentially through the processes of shared systematic inquiry. In the world of Peircean realism, therefore, one can experience God inferentially as Spirit, as a dynamic force, a vector, an interpretative tendency that lures human experience lovingly. To experience that divine lure one must cultivate affective and imaginative openness to the divine touch.[46]

Like aesthetics Peirce's other two normative sciences—ethics and logic—study the self-critical cultivation of other kinds of human habits. Ethics studies the habits of choice that orient us decisively to the ideals, realities, and values that make life worth living. Logic studies the habits of thought that allow us to perceive reality clearly so that we choose correctly those things that lead to the ideals, realities, and values that beautify life and make it worth living.[47]

Moreover, while Peirce conceived the pragmatic maxim originally as a principle of explanatory logic, he recognized that it has a role to play in normative thinking as well. The deductive explicitation of the practical consequences of a normative hypothesis clarifies it in a way that allows one to validate or invalidate it.

For example, the normative science of aesthetics studies the systematic cultivation of healthy affective responses to the real, responses that open the heart to the experience of genuine excellence. Clinical psychology, however, suggests that the systematic repression of negative human emotions like shame, guilt, fear, and anger has the opposite result. One can clarify the meaning of such a strictly normative hypothesis pragmatically: 1) by a developing predictive symptomology of the personality dysfunctions that result from habitually repressing negative emotions and 2) by suggesting therapeutic techniques for dealing with those dysfunctions. One validates or invalidates such an hypothesis by implementing the appropriate therapies in order to determine whether or not they foster emotional balance and aesthetic sensitivity.

An analogous use of pragmatic logic in normative thinking would call for a similar deductive clarification of ethical and logical hypotheses.

I find it theologically suggestive and interesting that Peirce's philosophy of the normative sciences anticipates in a significant way Bernard Lonergan's theology of conversion. In Lonergan's account of method in theology, the theology of conversion lays the foundations for the ongoing, inculturated reformulation of Christian faith. Moreover, Lonergan set the theological understanding of conversion on an entirely new footing when he suggested that conversion comes in more than one kind and that it can occur in secular as well as in religious contexts. Originally, Lonergan recognized only two forms of secular conversion: intellectual and moral. He subsequently conceded, however, the need to add a third: affective, or psychic, conversion, although he left it to other thinkers to explore its dynamics.[48]

In Lonergan's understanding of theological method, the functional theological specialty called "foundations" studies the experience of conversion. Like Peirce's normative sciences, foundational theology engages in strictly normative thinking. Moreover, interestingly enough, Lonergan's secular forms of conversion correlate with the very realms of experience that Peirce's normative sciences study.

For Lonergan the elaboration of a theology of conversion engages the same kind of thinking that Peirce called "normative." It demands critical self-understanding and yields insight into the kinds of realities, ideals, and values that ought to direct authentic human growth and development. Lonergan's affective conversion corresponds, therefore, to Peirce's normative science of aesthetics.

Lonergan's ethical conversion corresponds to Peirce's normative science of ethics. Lonergan's intellectual conversion corresponds to Peirce's normative science of logic.[49]

Lonergan's foundational method allows for pluralism in the study of conversion; but Lonergan gave very few hints about how to develop a foundational account of conversion other than to prescribe three sets of categories: transcendental, philosophical categories; special, faith-derived theological categories; and general theological categories derived from sciences, other than philosophy and theology, that study human experience.[50]

The correlation between Pierce's normative sciences and the secular forms of conversion suggests, however, a method for dissipating somewhat the vagueness in which Lonergan left foundational method.[51] A theology of affective conversion would do well to adopt the method of Peirce's aesthetics as a way of cultivating healthy affective perceptions of excellence. A theology of ethical conversion would do well to study the systematic cultivation of those habits of choice that orient life to the truth and goodness to which aesthetic experience gives appreciative access. A theology of intellectual conversion would do well to study the systematic cultivation of habits of thought that allow the human mind to perceive the world truly, so that one can choose wisely what enhances and beautifies human life.

Lonergan's theology of conversion complements Peirce's theory of the normative sciences, however, by making it clear that any adequate theology of conversion must, besides studying the secular forms of conversion, give an adequate normative account of how Christian conversion occurs and of how it transforms the other forms of conversion.

Finally, putting Peirce's philosophy of the normative sciences into dialogue with foundational theology in Lonergan's sense of that term bears theological fruit in another way. It does so by clarifying the relationship between orthodoxy and orthopraxis.

Here again we find an interesting convergence between Peirce's thought and Lonergan's. In Lonergan's study of method in theology, foundational theology begins the process of reconstructing theology after the functional specialties of mediating theology—research, interpretation, history, and dialectics—have effected the systematic retrieval of the Christian tradition.

Lonergan recognizes that any systematic study of the Christian tradition will reveal contradictory accounts of the message of Christianity and of the practical demands of Christian living. Lonergan also recognizes that, when confronted with the tangled and conflicting claims of the differing theologians, traditions, and churches, anyone engaged in the contemporary reconstruction of theology will need norms in order to distinguish sound doctrines from unsound doctrines. One will need, in other words, criteria for determining a particular doctrine's orthodoxy.

Lonergan finds the necessary norms in foundational theology, in a strictly normative account of the different kinds of conversion. In other words, in Lonergan's theory of theological method, orthopraxis, understood as a sound insight into the practical demands of affective, intellectual, moral, and religious conversion, supplies the fundamental norms for determining orthodoxy. Any doctrine that fosters integral conversion before God at an affective, intellectual, moral, and religious level counts as orthodox; any doctrine that fails to do so (or, worse, any doctrine that subverts such integral conversion) contradicts orthodox faith.[52]

Peirce's account of the relationship between the normative sciences and metaphysics anticipates and validates these insights of Lonergan. Peirce regarded proficiency in the three normative sciences as the pre-condition to doing metaphysics. By metaphysics he meant the science of the real. Moreover, Peirce judged that one needs to invoke the insights of all three normative sciences in order to grasp the nature of the real. Logic alone does not suffice. In other words, for Peirce the grasp of reality demands not only a well-ordered mind but a well-ordered conscience and a well-ordered affectivity as well. A well-ordered mind linked to a disordered conscience can all too easily invoke logic to rationalize situations of evil and injustice. A well-ordered mind linked to a disordered affectivity and to a disordered imagination can all too easily invoke logic in order to rationalize human neurosis and even psychosis. G.K. Chesterton once wisely remarked that a true madman has lost everything but his reason.

If one invokes Peirce's theory of the normative science in order to develop the method of foundational theology in Lonergan's sense of that term, it demands that the formulation of religious orthodoxy submit not only to criteria supplied by religious faith but also to criteria provided by the secular forms of conversion. In other words, the certification of orthodoxy demands that one distinguish sound doctrine from the religious rationalization of emotional pathology and of ethical irresponsibility, whether personal or institutional. The certification of orthodoxy also demands that a doctrine express sound logical and methodological presuppositions.

If both Peirce and Lonergan have the right of it (and I, for one, am inclined to think that on this issue they do), then we must understand orthopraxis as action rooted in a strictly normative insight into the practical demands not only of divine revelation but also of emotionally healthy, morally responsible, and intellectually truthful living. So understood, orthopraxis measures orthodoxy, not vice versa. Indeed, without the insights yielded by Peirce's normative sciences one lacks adequate means to distinguish sound religious teaching from the pious rationalization of personal and institutional pathology, moral hypocrisy, and deceit.

In the second and third sections of this chapter, we saw how pragmatic logic and epistemology call into question the presuppositions that ground Clodovis Boff's portrayal of theology as a purely theoretical science with only an accidental and extrinsic relationship to political praxis. The argument of this final section calls into question the dichotomy that Segundo introduces between speculative and evaluative thinking. Pragmatic logic demands that we recognize the evaluative as well as the normative character of explanatory thinking. It demands as well that one derive the criteria for grasping the truth about reality from strictly normative thinking about the practical demands of authentic living at an affective, moral, intellectual, and religious level.

Let me close by observing that the preceding account of the relationship between orthopraxis and orthodoxy provides a speculative justification for the claim of liberation theology that the sound reconstruction of theology demands a preferential option for the poor as an ethical pre-condition. Until one makes such an option, one has failed to recognize one of the fundamental moral demands of Christian conversion.53 If, however, the grasp of religious reality demands not only a well-ordered mind, but a well-ordered affectivity as well as a well-ordered conscience at both a personal and public level, then disorders in one's Christian conscience, like the failure to join Jesus in his preferential commitment to the poor, will with moral inevitability betray the reconstructive theologian into heterodoxy.

Notes

[1]Gustavo Gutierrez, **The Theology of Liberation: Revised Edition,** translated by Sister Caridad Inda and John Eagleson (Maryknoll: Orbis, 1988), p. xxxiv.

[2]Cornel West, **The American Evasion of Philosophy: A Genealogy of Pragmatism** (Madison: University of Wisconsin Press, 1989).

[3]**Ibid.,** pp. xxx, 5-12.

[4]**Ibid.,** pp. xxviii-ix, 5-12. In this context, one should note that in Gutierrez's thought, liberation theology understood as critical reflection on liberating Christian praxis supplements but does not replace two other major functions of theology: the cultivation of wisdom and the elaboration of a rational account of the faith (**Ibid.,** 4-5).

[5]**Ibid.,** pp. 17-22.

[6]**Ibid.,** pp. 43-46.

[7]Juan Luis Segundo, **The Liberation of Theology,** translated by John Drury (Maryknoll: Orbis, 1982), pp. 7-39.

[8]**Ibid.,** pp. 102-10, 154-82.

[9]**Ibid.,** pp. 8-9, 102, 106-10, 154-82.

[10]Juan Luis Segundo, **Faith and Ideologies** (Maryknoll: Orbis, 1982), p. 25.

[11]**Ibid.,** p. 27.

[12]**Ibid.,** pp. 17, 73-77, 105-06, 155, 163-7, 265-67. Cf. Donald L. Gelpi, S.J., **Inculturating North American Theology: An Experiment in Foundational Method** (Atlanta: Scholars Press, 1988), pp. 130-32, n. 11.

[13]Clodovis Boff, **Theology and Praxis: Epistemological Foundations,** translated by Robert Barr (New York: Orbis, 1987), pp. 5-62.

[14]**Ibid.,** pp. 5-6.

[15]**Ibid.,** pp. 195-97.

[16]**Ibid.,** pp. 17, 29-34, 45-48, 71-72.

[17]**Ibid.,** pp. 213-16.

[18]**Ibid.,** pp. 206-19.

[19]**Ibid.,** pp. 206-16.

[20]Richard Bernstein, **Praxis and Action: Contemporary Philosophies of Human Activity** (Philadelphia: University of Pennsylvania Press, 1971), pp. xiii-v.

[21]Murray G. Murphy, **The Development of Peirce's Philosophy** (Cambridge: Harvard University Press, 1961), pp. 16-17, 32-51.

[22]Charles Sanders Peirce, **Collected Papers,** edited by Charles Hartshorne and Paul Weiss (8 vols.; Cambridge: Harvard University Press, 1931-58), 1.4-6.

[23]Peirce, **op. cit.,** 5.266-82.

[24]**Ibid.,** 6.428-93.

[25]In **Insights and Illusions of Philosophy** Jean Piaget mounts a similar critique of modern European theories of knowledge. Philosophers, Piaget argues, rest content with formulating hypotheses about how people think. Until philosophers attempt to validate or invalidate their theories through the psychological investigation of human thought processes, they will continue to offer only unverified abductions about human thinking. Cf. Jean Piaget, **Insights and Illusions of Philosophy,** translated by Wolfe Mays (New York: World, 1971).

[26]Francis E. Reilly, S.J., **Charles Peirce's Theory of Scientific Method** (New York: Fordham University Press, 1970), pp. 23-77.

[27]Charles Sanders Peirce, **Collected Papers,** edited by Charles Hartshorne and Paul Weiss (8 vols.; Cambridge: Harvard University Press, 1934), 5.402.

[28]**Ibid.,** 1.6, 93-119, 180-212.

[29]**Ibid.,** 6.246-71.

[30]**Ibid.,** 5.15-26.

[31]**Ibid.,** 5.358-87.

[32]**Ibid.,** 5.41-65, 82-91.

[33]**Ibid.,** 6.238-271.

[34]For a further development of this suggestion, see Donald L. Gelpi, S.J., "Thematic Grace vs. Transmuting Grace: Two Spiritual Paths," in **Grace as Transmuted Experience and Social Process: and Other Essays in North American Theology** (Lanham: University Press of America, 1988), pp. 67-95.

[35]John Dewey, **Logic: The Theory of Inquiry** (New York: Holt, Reinhart, and Winston, 1938), pp. 23-31. The psychology of Jean Piaget lends inductive validation to this aspect of Dewey's thought. Cf. John H. Flavell, **The Developmental Psychology of Jean Piaget** (New York: Van Nostrand, 1963).

[36]**Ibid.,** pp. 33-41.

[37]**Ibid.,** pp. 66-71.

[38]**Ibid.,** pp. 104-05.

[39]**Ibid.,** pp. 105-11.

[40]**Ibid.,** pp. 121-23, 131-38, 159-72.

[41]For a lucid study of this dimension of Dewey's thought, see Robert Roth, **John Dewey and Self-Realization** (Englewood Cliffs: Prentice-Hall, Inc., 1962).

[42]Bernard Lonergan, **Method in Theology** (New York: Herder and Herder, 1972), xi-xii, 125-45.

[43]Peirce, **op. cit.,** 5.41-44.

[44]**Ibid.,** 5.34-40, 69-93. For a lucid treatment of Peirce's theory of the normative sciences, cf. Vincent Potter, **Charles S. Peirce on Norms and Ideals** (Worcester: University of Massachusetts Press, 1967).

[45]**Ibid.,** 6.452-457.

[46]In point of fact, Josiah Royce in his mature philosophy of religion would develop this aspect of Peirce's thought; but he would do so with Peirce's approval. Cf. Frank M. Oppenheim, **Royce's Mature Philosophy of Religion** (Notre Dame: University of Notre Dame Press, 1987).

[47]Peirce, **op. cit.,** 5.34-40, 129-50.

[48]Lonergan, **Method in Theology,** pp. 237-47.

[49]**Ibid.,** pp. 267-69.

[50]**Ibid.,** pp. 271-93.

[51]For a more detailed account of the methods of foundational thinking, see Donald L. Gelpi, S.J., **Inculturating North American Theology: An Experiment in Foundational Method** (Atlanta: Scholars Press, 1988).

[52]**Ibid.,** pp. 295-333.

[53]For a more detailed discussion of this point, see Donald L. Gelpi, S.J., **Grace as Transmuted Experience and Social Process: and Other Essays in North American Theology** (Lanham: University Press of America, 1988), pp. 97-139.

3

The Turn to Experience in Process Theology

Among contemporary theological movements, process theology has made the turn to experience more systematically than any other. Process theology attempts to exploit Alfred North Whitehead's philosophy of organism in a theological context. Most process theologians read Whitehead with the aid of his most systematic commentator: Charles Hartshorne.[1] Hartshorne developed Whitehead's di-polar theism more systematically than Whitehead himself; but Whitehead created the intellectual world in which process theologians have elected to dwell.

In this chapter I shall attempt to assess the results of process theology's turn to experience. My argument divides into two parts. In the first part, I shall examine Whitehead's system in the light of his own method. In the second part of my argument, I shall reflect on what happens to Christian revelation when one attempts to think it within the nominalistic confines of Whitehead's universe.

In what follows, I shall be voicing some serious criticisms of Whitehead's philosophical system. Let me then begin with a word of positive appreciation for Whitehead's accomplishment; for without any doubt he holds a major place among the Anglo-American philosophers of this century. My own scholarly work owes much to his creativity and vision.

As I have already written elsewhere, I find much to commend in Whitehead's philosophical project. I find his criticisms of a Cartesian or Lockean notion of substance sound. I concur in his portrayal of the spatio-temporal realities as self-defining processes. I believe that he correctly conceives the subject of change as the product of change rather than its substrate. I found his critique of essentialism fundamentally sound as well as his suggestion that one can define adequately what a thing is only by recapitulating its entire history. I like his insistence on the relational character of reality and his conception of individuality as qualitative rather than as purely quantitative. I like his equation of Being and process. Like him, I aspire to developing a metaphysics of experience and would defend a type of panentheism. I endorse Whitehead's attempt to portray God in a dialogic relationship with creation, and I resonate with his vision of a God who lures his creatures rather than coerces them.[2]

I could develop the preceding list of Whiteheadean virtues and insights in considerable detail; but time, space, and the topic of this book preclude such a development. This book examines inadequacies in the contemporary theological turn to experience. I know that in writing such a book I run the risk of sounding negative and carping; but I have only positive intentions. Only when contemporary theologians recognize the inadequacies in philosophical constructs of experience that they invoke will theology make a fruitful turn to experience.

I would hope that the reader would keep these things in mind in the course of what follows. In what follows, however, I shall focus on what I regard as problematic issues in Whitehead's thought, issues that call for serious criticism and that process theologians have to date tended to ignore. I shall try to treat Whitehead with complete fairness. In criticizing his system I shall not invoke any principle that he himself did not endorse. In fact, I would like to think that in all that follows I shall say nothing about Whitehead's system that he himself would not admit were he alive today.

(I)

Whitehead did not see himself as a theologian. Indeed, Whitehead looked to philosophy rather than to theology to provide religion with its intellectual content.[3] Moreover, as we shall see, much process theology advances with the same presupposition, since process theologians tend to assume, often naively, that

Whitehead's philosophical system supplies the content of the Christian gospel.

As we have seen in reflecting on the turn to experience in liberation theology, Clodovis Boff uses the term "praxis" as a quasi-metaphysical term and defines that term in much the same way that Schillebeeckx defines the term "experience." Whitehead, however, makes the turn to experience more systematically than any of the thinkers we have examined heretofore because he transforms the term "experience" into a formal metaphysical category universally applicable in intent. Moreover, he does so in the course of developing a cosmology that aspires to logical rigor, coherence, applicability, and adequacy.

Logical rigor demands that Whitehead's system not contradict itself. Coherence demands that all the key terms in that system imply one another in such a way as to defy understanding when abstracted from the others. Applicability demands that the system interpret some realities. Adequacy demands that there be no realities it cannot interpret.[4]

Whitehead recognized the fallibility of his philosophy. He realized that in writing **Process and Reality** he had enunciated the most fallible of hypotheses: a world-hypothesis, an account of the nature of the universe in general. He envisaged the possibility that his system would prove inadequate to the facts either in minor correctable details or completely. Moreover, in invoking the criteria of logical rigor and coherence, he also conceded the possibility that he may have contradicted himself.[5]

Whitehead makes the turn to experience in enunciating his "reformed subjectivist principle." The reformed subjectivist principle states "that apart from the experiences of subjects there is nothing, nothing, nothing, bare nothingness."[6] When, however, Whitehead speaks of "the experiences of subjects," he does not mean that the subject has the experience but that the subject is the experience; for Whitehead rejects the notion of substance and with it the idea that anything underlies experience.[7] Moreover, Whitehead also conceives each emerging subject as constituted by its own feelings, whether physical or conceptual.[8] In a sense, the philosophy of organism revises Descartes' "I think, therefore I am" to read "I experience, therefore I am."

The reformed subjectivist principle rejects the idea of vacuous actuality. By "vacuous actuality" Whitehead means the mechanistic universe of Newton and Descartes. Instead of conceiving physical reality as a machine devoid of evaluative response, Whitehead discovers evaluation at the heart of every physical process, even of the most minute atomic and subatomic reactions. In truth, the insertion of an evaluative response into every physical process explains in part why Whitehead chooses to call his system a philosophy of organism; for it allows him to trace a continuity of development from the most minute physical processes to the highest forms of organic life and conceptual thought.[9]

Whitehead, however, invokes much the same di-polar construct of experience as Schillebeeckx does in his theological turn to experience and as Clodovis Boff does in his metaphysical account of the meaning of praxis. As a consequence, moreover, Whitehead falls into the same kind of conceptual nominalism as they. Whitehead, however, with the logical consistency and systematic flair he so admired, elaborates the di-polarity of his construct of experience, both its subjectivity, and its nominalistic character, in greater conceptual detail.

Whitehead constructs experience out of the subjective interrelationship of physical and conceptual feelings. He characterizes physical feelings as concrete, actual, and determinate and conceptual feelings as particular.[10] A world constructed from concrete physical facts and particular, abstract conceptions, however, lacks any real generality. In other words, it stands alongside other post-Cartesian, nominalistic accounts of human experience.

Whitehead insists on the subjectivity of experience in the course of elaborating his "Category of Freedom and Determination." The Category of Freedom and Determination states that "the concrescence of each individual actual entity is internally determined and externally free."[11]

By an actual entity Whitehead means "a final reality or **res vera.**"[12] As we have just seen, however, the Reformed Subjectivist Principle equates reality with "experience"; and experience consists in the interrelation of concrete, physical feelings and particular conceptual feelings. In Whitehead's universe, as experience grows, decision transforms particular ideas, or possibilities, into wholly determinate and concrete physical realities. The development of experience, its "concrescence," implies, therefore, both the harmonizing, the growing together, of concrete facts and abstract possibilities and the reduction of an instance of experience to physical concreteness.

The Category of Freedom and Determination, moreover, requires that concrescences advance in such a way that the emerging actual entity remains "internally determined and externally free." By that Whitehead means that every actual entity, every occasion of experience, determines itself to become what it wants to become by its own subjective decision. The state of the universe at the emergence of each occasion of experience conditions what it can become, as do the possibilities to which it related. Nevertheless, each occasion of experience, and it alone, creates itself. In other words, in Whitehead's construct of experience, the interrelation of concrete, physical feelings and abstract, conceptual possibilities transpires entirely within the self-creative subjectivity of each actual entity. As each occasion of experience creates itself subjectively, it remains impervious to outside influence.

Whitehead derives his conceptual nominalism from two American sources: from William James and from George Santayana. In the preface to **Process and Reality**, Whitehead acknowledges his indebtedness to Bergson, James, and Dewey.[13]

While one can, I believe, absolve Dewey from having defended a nominalistic construct of experience, James derived his conceptual nominalism in part from Bergson, who also conceived of cognition as the interrelation of concrete percepts and abstract concepts. The early James, the James of **The Principles of Psychology**, recognized the role that habit plays in experience, but he explained the reality of habit, not by appealing to real generality, but by ascribing it to the plasticity of matter.[14] James, moreover, included within percepts not only concrete sensible things but concrete actions and relationships. He described the latter as feelings of tendency. Nevertheless, lifelong immersion in the tradition of

British empiricism finally led the mature James to conceive of experience as nominalistically as John Locke. In **Some Problems in Philosophy**, James' last and posthumously published work, he describes experience as the subjective interrelation of concrete percepts and abstract concepts. The mature James also held that experience develops in atomic drops.[15] Whitehead endorsed both of these positions.[16]

George Santayana's **Skepticism and Animal Faith** influenced significantly Whitehead's theory of prehensions.[17] By a "prehension" Whitehead means a concrete fact of relatedness, a concrescent drop of experience. Every prehension contains: 1) a subject that does the prehending or relating, 2) what it prehends, and 3) the way it prehends it.[18]

Moreover, Whitehead cites Santayana repeatedly in **Process and Reality**, almost always favorably.[19] Small wonder, since in **Skepticism and Animal Faith** Santayana lays the speculative foundations for a Platonic, conceptual nominalism much like Whitehead's. Santayana develops his nominalistic metaphysics systematically in his **Realms of Being**. Santayana's realm of essence corresponds to Whitehead's realm of eternal objects. Santayana's realm of matter corresponds to Whitehead's physical feelings. Whitehead transforms Santayana's animal faith into his doctrine of prehension. Both men conceived the world nominalistically as the subjective interrelation of concrete percepts and abstract concepts.

Like Kant, however, and in contrast to Whitehead, Santayana recognizes that a systematically developed nominalism makes the experience of God impossible. He therefore refuses to follow Whitehead in confusing the novel essences the human mind knows with ideas in the mind of God. I shall return to this point later.

The roots of Whitehead's nominalism run much deeper, however, than James, Bergson, and Santayana. Whitehead derives the inspiration for his philosophy of organism from the most articulate conceptual nominalists of the seventeenth and eighteenth centuries: Descartes, Locke, Hume, and Kant. In **Process and Reality** he writes:

A more detailed discussion of Descartes, Locke, and Hume—
in this and in the succeeding chapter—may make plain how
deeply the philosophy of organism is founded on seventeenth-
century thought and how at certain critical points it diverges
from that thought.[20]

At what "critical points" does Whitehead diverge from these
classical nominalistic epistemologies? Whitehead criticizes
Descartes, Locke, and Hume on two major points: their acquiescence in a substance-quality doctrine of reality and their omission
of a physical component from their account of experience. He also
criticizes Kant for trying to construct an objective world exclusively from subjective experience[21] and for beginning his theory of
knowledge with the critique of pure reason instead of with aesthetics.[22] Whitehead does not, however, criticize the conceptualism of
these four thinkers. On the contrary, he endorses it together with
the nominalism that it implies.

I have suggested that process theology offers an interesting
case study of the attempt to conceive religious experience nominalistically, because it employs a more systematically developed nominalism than any of the theologians we have considered heretofore.
As a consequence, a critical examination of process thought
demonstrates in greater clarity and detail not only that nominalism
fails to explain Christian religious experience but also that it fails
to explain much of ordinary natural human experience as well.

Without a doubt, Whitehead proposes a dynamic construct of
reality. He equates reality with process, with the result that anything not in process ceases by that very fact to exist. Nevertheless,
if one applies to Whitehead's system the methodological criteria of
logical rigor and coherence that he used to formulate it, one has
reason to question his system's ability to explain the reality of
process.

In Whitehead's system the category "creativity" functions as
the category of "the ultimate."[23] By "the ultimate" Whitehead
means "the universal of universals."[24] In other words, whatever
exists must exemplify creativity as Whitehead defines the term.
Ultimacy for Whitehead has then primarily logical connotations. In

asserting the universal predictability of "creativity," however, Whitehead also makes an important statement about the nature of the real. In effect, Whitehead is portraying all reality as self-creative.

The principle of coherence demands, moreover, that one interpret the meaning of the category "creativity" in the light of the other key categories in Whitehead's categoreal scheme. For example, the reformed subjectivist principle, as we have just seen, equates being and experience. By the principle of coherence, it follows that in the world of Whitehead, every experience exemplifies creativity and vice versa. Similarly, the universal predictability of "creativity" means that one should find it predicable of all the other categories in Whitehead's categoreal scheme. Moreover, because they exemplify creativity, they explain it, not it them.

By Whitehead's other categories, I mean his categories of existence, his categories of explanation, and his categoreal obligations. The categories of existence describe the elements that combine in creativity; the categories of explanation describe how they combine; the categoreal obligations enunciate the principles that govern their combining. These categories explain creativity; it does not explain them. Instead, it exemplifies them. As we shall see, in the section that follows, more than one process theologian has failed to understand the way "creativity" functions in relationship to the other categories and has fallaciously used it as a category of explanation rather than as the category of the ultimate.

Whitehead defines "creativity" as "the advance from disjunction to conjunction, creating a novel entity other than the entities given in disjunction."[25] In other words, creativity demands that every individual drop of experience organize itself into a novel concrescence of feeling.

When, however, one applies the methodological criterion of coherence to the term "creativity," one begins, I believe, to run into problems of logical consistency that violate the criterion of logical rigor. By invoking the criterion of coherence, Whitehead clearly wants the categories of existence and of explanation as well as his categoreal obligations to explain why creativity happens. It seems to me, however, that those very categories fail finally to explain convincingly that precise point. Let me explain what I mean.

In the world of Whiteheadean conceptual nominalism each drop of experience must create itself from a wholly determinate, concrete, physical feeling and from particular, abstract concepts, or conceptual feelings. Whitehead recognizes that an abstract concept can effect nothing. He therefore ascribes efficacy to the physical pole of experience; but he never explains how a wholly determinate, concrete, physical feeling can do anything other than just be wholly determinate, concrete, and physical. Just calling a totally determined perished fact a feeling does not endow it with efficacy in reality. Nor does calling it an emotion solve the problem. The problem stems both from the complete determination of physical feelings and from the fact that each drop of experience in Whitehead's scheme must perish before another drop of experience can replace it. A totally determined, perished fact—say, the fact that I just turned off the lights on leaving my office—remains everlastingly true; but it cannot do anything because the action no longer exists as a fact. It has passed into history and exists in memory alone. In Whitehead's terms, it has achieved objective immortality.

Perished facts, even when we call them emotions and physical feelings, explain nothing. On the contrary, a concrete, determined event needs explanation by the law or laws that cause it. Here, I believe, Peirce, in invoking a triadic rather than a di-polar construct of experience, saw more deeply into nature than Whitehead did. In other words, because Whitehead does not acknowledge the existence of laws in the strict sense, i.e. of general tendencies to act or evaluate in specific ways, his categoreal scheme has no way of explaining why process, creativity, happens at all. The juxtaposition within experience of a totally determinate, past physical reality with an inert possibility produces in the last analysis nothing at all but the juxtaposition in experience of a totally determinate fact and an inert and inefficacious possibility. Neither in itself has the capacity to do anything other than to be what it is. Hence, their juxtaposition makes nothing happen.

Whitehead's discussion of the laws of nature as immanent, as imposed, and as observed order of succession illustrates his failure to grasp Peirce's category of "thirdness," or real generality. By law as immanent, Whitehead means the essences, the eternal objects, concretely ingredient in things. Imposed laws mean that things in nature have to enter into relationship with other constituents of nature. By these other constituents, Whitehead seems to mean the eternal objects in the mind of God viewed as the ultimate source of the order in nature. By law as observed succession, Whitehead would seem to mean a nexus, a describable pattern of natural events.[26]

Nor does God's assigning a subjective aim to an occasion of experience get things going. A subjective aim can lure teleologically, but it can effect nothing.[27] Efficacy in Whitehead's universe must derive from the physical pole of experience; but a totally determined physical reality, a past fact that in Whitehead's terms enjoys "objective immortality," in and of itself can effect nothing. It can only continue to be what it is. That plus the absence of real generality from Whitehead's conceptual scheme seems to me to leave "creativity" inexplicable in terms of the other categories and convicts Whitehead's categoreal scheme of a major logical contradiction.

To sum up, then, what I have been saying, the rest of Whitehead's categories—his categories of existence, his categories of explanation, and his categoreal obligations—cannot finally explain his category of the ultimate, even though the principle of coherence requires that they do. Since the categories of existence describe a nominalistic universe, they present a construct of experience in which nothing can happen in principle. As a consequence, the categories of explanation have, in the last analysis, nothing to explain. Similarly, in a nominalistic world without laws, a world utterly devoid of real generality, the categoreal obligations lack any grounding in reality. Because past physical facts as past can only continue to be what they are, Whitehead's categoreal scheme cannot explain why, on the perishing of an occasion of experience, any other drop of experience should come into existence. In the world of conceptual nominalism, creativity itself forfeits all creative potential because it lacks the real generality that grounds and validates normative explanations of events.

Whitehead's nominalism leads him into other speculative impasses. Whitehead certainly insisted on the interrelatedness of all things and that every decision changes the shape of the universe. Moreover, process theologians correctly praise Whitehead for having proposed a thoroughly relational account of God and of reality.

Nevertheless, for all its talk of universal organic interrelatedness, Whitehead's philosophy, in my judgment, fails finally to meet Whitehead's own criterion of adequacy. By that I mean that Whitehead's categoreal scheme lacks the conceptual wherewithal to explain the fundamental experience of interpersonal relationship, the sort of relationship that Martin Buber called an I-Thou relationship. Let me explain what I mean.

Whitehead does speak of the primacy of relationship; but on closer scrutiny **Process and Reality** offers, in my judgment, a very underdeveloped account of relationship, a deficiency that process theologians have tended systematically to ignore. Two factors in Whitehead's thought combine to prevent his speculative account of relationship from enjoying the logical adequacy that he wanted it to have: the abstract, mathematical way in which he conceived of relationship and the atomicity of experience. Let us reflect on each of these dimensions of Whitehead's philosophy in turn.

In Whitehead's universe relationship consists of a reified geometrical grid concretized in each atomic drop of experience. Whitehead calls this grid "the extensive continuum" and insists that it exists only as an aspect of the drops of experience that atomize it.[28] These drops of experience, however, create themselves entirely through decision. Moreover, once a drop of experience makes conceptual feelings concrete through decision, it perishes. In Whitehead's terms, it achieves objective immortality by becoming a past fact. All of this allegedly occurs in a fraction of a second.[29]

Whitehead insists on the atomic character of each drop of experience. Moreover, the atomicity of experience means that in Whitehead's universe nothing can move. Whitehead's cosmology rules out the possibility of physical motion in principle.[30] Whitehead observes: "Thus an actual entity never moves: it is where it is and what it is. In order to emphasize this characteristic by a phrase connecting the motion of 'actual entity' more closely with our ordinary habits of thought, I will also use the term 'actual occasion' in the place of the term 'actual entity.'"[31]

Whitehead, of course, realizes that things seem to move but dismisses the appearance of motion as an illusion. What we call motion, he suggests, really consists of a series of overlapping atomic occasions of experience that come to be and perish in a fraction of a second. They appear to move to the eye but in fact do not move any more than a series of blinking lights on a theater marquee actually move as the lights flash successively. In contrast to the blinking lights, moreover, the overlapping of occasions makes the illusion of motion all the more effective, although how a new experience overlaps with a perished one remains something of a mystery.[32]

This paradoxical explanation of the appearance but non-existence of real motion also illustrates the logical inadequacy of Whitehead's conceptual nominalism. Laws provide experience not only with real generality but with real continuity within development. Because Whitehead's system lacks any category of real generality, it also has no means to explain real continuity within development. As a result, experience fragments into a series of overlapping drops immovably rooted in a particular fragment of space.

Moreover, in my judgment, the transferral of the same subjective aim from one drop of experience to another within a society, or "nexus," of actual occasions fails finally to explain the reality of continuity within experience, although some Whiteheadeans allege that it does. I take this stand, because the atomicity and physical immobility of experience (its lack, in the last analysis, of any real continuity) mean that transferral of the same aim from one occasion of experience to another also creates only an illusion of continuity, not the reality of continuity.

As a consequence of the atomicity and physical immobility of experience, the next drop of experience must wait until another entity has perished, has turned itself into a totally determinate, objective, physical fact and has thus achieved objective immortality. Only then can the new drop of experience enter into relationship with the perished entity, or, in Whitehead's terms, prehend it. When that happens, however, the new emerging entity grasps the perished reality merely as a datum for its processing, as factually given. In other words, in Buber's terms, one Whiteheadean entity can have a factual, utilitarian I-It relationship with another by prehending it as a datum for its own processing; but it cannot have an existential I-Thou relationship, since existential relationships transcend the utilitarian.[33] It follows therefore that in Whitehead's nominalistic universe, one can ingest physical facts but one cannot relate to persons as persons.

Given the inadequacy of Whitehead's philosophy of relationship, it comes as no great surprise that, despite the richness of Whitehead's system in other respects, it leaves the concept "person" woefully underdeveloped. Whitehead defines the term "person" in objectified, impersonal categories as "an enduring object."[34]

Whether Whitehead's God qualifies as a person remains problematic. Nor does one relate personally to Whitehead's God. One experiences God through "reversion," i.e. through the prehension of a novel possibility in the mind of God.[35] Whitehead, however, describes that experience, not as an interpersonal encounter, but in impersonal terms as the apperception of a "private matter of fact."[36] That Whitehead would conceive of an idea, an eternal object as a "private matter of fact," underscores the nominalistic character of his position. He conceived even ideas as enjoying the quasi-facticity and concreteness that he called particularity.

Whitehead's failure to explain human social relationships with logical adequacy derives from another serious deficiency in his system: namely, his transformation of an individual into a society of actual occasions, what Whitehead calls a "nexus."[37] Paradoxically, Whitehead uses the term "society," not to describe persons in relationship but in order to designate an individual experience prolonged in space and time. Indeed, the category of freedom and determination, which demands that each drop of experience in every nexus create itself subjectively, rules out in principle social experience as human persons normally enjoy and conceive it; for interaction creates the social bonds among persons. In other words, in Whitehead's theory of experience, despite his affirmation of the universal geometrical relatedness of all things, his category of freedom and determination transforms the turn to the subject into something approaching social solipsism.

In other words, Whitehead's decision to use the term "society" to designate individuals combines with the atomicity and immobility of his understanding of experience in order to deprive his categoreal scheme of the ability to describe with any clarity or conviction what we normally mean by human social relationships. To put the matter concretely, in the nominalistic world of concrescing drops of experience, one has no way finally to describe the familiar human experience of one person conversing with one friend about another. In this respect, Whitehead's categoreal scheme fails to measure up to its own norm of adequacy.

Similarly, Whitehead's categoreal scheme has no adequate language to describe human social institutions. Unfortunately more than one process theologian has assumed, incorrectly in my estimate, that Whitehead's account of what he calls "societies" extends to human social and political structures. In point of fact, however, what Whitehead calls a society most people call an individual. When he speaks of democratically organized societies, he means a rock or a jellyfish. When he speaks of a monarchically organized society, he means a dog or a cat or a human. Having squandered social categories on individuals, Whitehead's system lacks the conceptual capital to develop either a philosophy of society or a political philosophy in the traditional understanding of society and politics. Whitehead correctly describes his system as a cosmology; it probes the order of nature and has little or nothing finally to say about the structure of human society.[38]

Whitehead himself, of course, delighted in reflecting on the course of human history. Both **Science and the Modern World** and **Adventures of Ideas** reveal a highly cultured mind interested in a broad spectrum of ideas and issues. His philosophical system, however, probably combined with his personal intellectual interests in order to focus his historical reflections primarily on the history of ideas. Among the ideas he discusses, one occasionally finds political concepts; but when one examines Whitehead's own categoreal scheme one finds it singularly bereft of categories that deal adequately with social and political realities in the normal sense of those terms.

I have been arguing that Whitehead's categoreal scheme fails its own test of adequacy when it attempts to talk about persons, human interpersonal relationships, and institutional structures. One may, I believe, make a similar criticism of Whitehead's theism.

To his great credit, Whitehead undertakes to reconcile belief in God and commitment to modern science. Unfortunately, however, Whitehead grounds his theism on a conceptual nominalism. Moreover, his conceptual nominalism prevents him, in my judgment, from providing an adequate account of human religious experience. Here too, I believe, the categoreal scheme does not measure up to its own norm of adequacy.

As we have seen already, theistic nominalists cannot find God at the concrete, sensible pole of experience, because they recognize that one cannot reduce God to a created fact. As a consequence, they must turn to the conceptual pole of experience in the hope of encountering God there. As we have also seen, in the case of Schillebeeckx, the attempt to find God at the conceptual pole of experience led him to ground resurrection faith in an inference based on a subjective feeling of salvation. In Whitehead's case, the search for God in the world of concepts ends in ontologism.

Whitehead constructs God's experience out of physical and conceptual feelings in a manner analogous to finite, created experience, although Whitehead's God allegedly processes from the conceptual rather than from the physical pole of experience. God's "primordial nature" designates the divine prehension of the totality of possibility, the evaluative grasp of every possible particular concept arranged in a preferential order of relevance to the creative process.[39] The physical world supplies the divine experience with its concrete, factual pole.[40] God's "superject nature" designates God as conditioning the world's future by offering it new, particular possibilities for development, although in the world of nominalism how God can act without exemplifying real generality remains as much a mystery as does the activity of creatures.[41]

In Whitehead's world, then, religious experience boils down to the experience of "reversion," to the immediate apprehension by a creature of an eternal object, a subjective matter of fact, a concept in the mind of God.[42] This ontologistic explanation of human cognition flows logically from Whitehead's nominalism. Because Whitehead conceives of the world's activity as purely physical, embodied, and concrete, he can discover in the created universe no grounds for novel conceptual thinking, which grasps disembodied possibilities. He therefore postulates a transcendent source of novel insight by locating them in the mind of God.

With Thomas Aquinas, I find this Platonized account of human conceptual activity inherently implausible. The human mind thinks its own thoughts; it does not think with the thoughts of God. Rather, the generation of novel thinking engages finite conceptual habits and involves neurological activity.

Moreover, it also comes as no surprise that a philosophical system that cannot account adequately for human interpersonal encounters also lacks the ability to describe the encounter with God in interpersonal terms. In the world of Whitehead, religious experience boils down to the subjective experience of a particular, novel concept or concepts, nothing more. The experience of a novel concept, however, falls woefully far short of describing an encounter with a transcendent personal reality. Moreover, by reducing religious experience to thinking a novel concept, Whitehead's system offers no categories even to describe, much less explain, the unitive, transconceptual knowledge of God of which the mystics speak.

Whitehead's system also completely naturalizes the relationship of God and creature. It does so by making God and the world so mutually interdependent that the Christian notion of grace as the free and gratuitous gift of God loses conceptual intelligibility. Whitehead cannot even conceive of creation as a gratuitous divine gift, since God and the world create one another. In other words, Whitehead's God needs the world in order to become God.

Here Whitehead's cosmology contrasts sharply with Christian

revelation. In Christian revelation, God, who exists from all eternity, need not have created. Having chosen to create a world, God lay under no obligation to undo the consequences of human sinfulness by becoming incarnate. Christian theology can, I believe, legitimately conceive of both creation and incarnation as free and gratuitous acts of divine self-limitation. Having decided to create a world in order to enter into a loving relationship with his creatures, the Christian God subsequently needs human collaboration to accomplish his saving ends; but the Christian God does not need the world's collaboration in order to become God. Instead, both creation and salvation count as God's utterly free and gratuitous gift. Moreover, they count as different kinds of gift.

In Whitehead's universe, by contrast, the world enables God to become God, at the same time that God enables the world to become the world. As Whitehead observes in the closing paragraphs of **Process and Reality,** "It is as true to say that God creates the World, as that the World creates God."[43] In other words, in a Whiteheadean cosmology, God cannot relate to the world in free and gratuitous love because God needs the world in order to achieve the satisfactions that make God God and therefore constitute the very reality of the divine experience.[44]

Finally, as we shall see in the section that follows, Whitehead's reduction of experience to immobile, atomic drops deprives it of categories needed to describe the eschatological dimensions of Christian experience. The fact that a Whiteheadean drop of experience comes into being and perishes in a fraction of a second endows it with a felt past and present. It feels its past by prehending the perished drop of experience with which it overlaps and which it incorporates into itself. The conceptual pole of experience endows it with "presentational immediacy" and thus endows it with an experienced present. Since, however, every drop of experience perishes within a fraction of a second, its "future" lies outside the drop of experience itself. Its future, what Whitehead calls its "superjective nature," consists of the other drops of experience that arise from it in the historical succession of experiences that Whitehead calls a nexus, a society of actual occasions. Remember that for Whitehead a nexus means an enduring object. Once the last drop of experience in any given nexus perishes, the entire nexus perishes. It no longer has a future and exists only with "objective immortality," as an idea in the mind of God.

In other words, the atomicity of experience combines with the denial of motion in order to preclude the possibility that any given actual occasion experiences the future as such. By the same token, the perpetual perishing of actual occasions renders both the idea of personal continuity and the idea of personal survival after death problematic in a Whiteheadean universe. When in the section that follows we examine W. Norman Pittenger's eschatology, we shall find that he recognizes this deficiency in Whitehead with grim fatalism.

I have been reflecting on some of the logical contradictions and inadequacies that result from Whitehead's acquiescence in a nominalistic construct of experience. In the course of these reflections, I have tried to apply Whitehead's own methodological presuppositions to his own categoreal scheme. The time has come to reflect on the speculative results achieved by process theologians in their attempt to employ this problematic philosophy as a vehicle for Christian theological thought.

Not everything that goes by the name of process theology deals, however, with Christian doctrine. Much of the literature reads more like philosophy than theology. In the section that follows, I shall therefore restrict my attention to the formally theological writings of contemporary process theologians, i.e. to systematic attempts to think traditional Christian beliefs in a Whiteheadean frame of reference.

(II)

Process theology emerged in this country as the response of liberal Protestant theology to the "death-of-God" movement. Process theologians conceded that the God of classical metaphysics had indeed died but did not mourn his demise because they believed that Whitehead's God had superseded him as the new, scientifically and philosophically updated God of metaphysics. One senses in the writings of many process theologians a Kierkegaardean leap when they abandon classical metaphysics for Whiteheadean theism. They leap, however, not into faith but into rationalism. In many ways, I find their loyalty to Whitehead touching, but I would take them more seriously as speculative theologians if they showed a willingness to subject Whitehead's system to a more systematic philosophical critique.

Many process theologians tend to assume either that Whitehead is describing the God of Christian revelation or that his philosophy finally provides Christian revelation with its content. This kind of liberal theological rationalism led Karl Barth to excommunicate philosophers from the theological enterprise. Barth's position dramatizes a perennial tendency in the Protestant theological tradition. Originally rooted in a pessimistic Augustinian view of human nature, much Protestant theology has tended historically to veer between the extremes of fideism and rationalism.

Sound theological method lies, however, somewhere between those extremes. The failure to incorporate critical philosophical reflection into the theological enterprise leaves speculative theologians prone to acquiesce uncritically in the illegitimate rational presuppositions they bring to the theological thinking. Nevertheless, in all that concerns the reality of God, divine self-revelation passes judgment on fallible human philosophical hypotheses, not vice versa.

Much Protestant process theology, by contrast, advances in the tradition of Protestant liberalism. It uses Whitehead's nominalistic cosmology as a Procrustean bed that measures the truth of Christian revelation. Whatever doesn't fit inside Whitehead's cosmological system gets lopped off as mythic or as rationally unjustifiable.

Process Christology illustrates what I mean. W. Norman Pittenger, David Griffin, and John B. Cobb have all formulated "process Christologies." In point of fact, all three have only constructed Jesusologies that so naturalize the understanding of divine grace as to make Christology unthinkable.

Pittenger made the first effort. Writing in the late 1950s, Pittenger rejected Chalcedonian Christology on the grounds that an "enhypostatic" understanding of the incarnation implied an "anhypostatic" interpretation of the humanity of Jesus. Pittenger derided Protestant neo-orthodox Christology for portraying the incarnation as "a bolt from the blue." Nothing would satisfy Pittenger but a restatement of Christology within the nominalistic confines of Whitehead's philosophy of organism. Pittenger described the Christian God's relation to the world in the same organic terms Whitehead had. When God and the world create one another, then, Pittenger insisted, they stand in a friendly collaborative relationship that allows one to conceive the presence of God in Jesus in more immanent terms than Barth's alleged "bolt from the blue." Just as Whitehead's God exemplifies the same laws as does the space-time process, so too Pittenger's Jesus simply exemplifies the divine action present in every drop of processing experience. In other words, Pittenger reduces the action of divine grace to "reversion," to God's offering to Jesus novel possibilities for growth and development in the same way that God does to every occasion of experience. In Jesus, we find someone who collaborated with God more successfully than anybody else. Jesus, therefore, confronts us as "supreme among all historic revealers and revelations of God."[45] Pittenger, however, offers no doctrinal, historical, or empirical justification for regarding Jesus as the supreme exemplification of Whiteheadean creativity. He just asserts it dogmatically.

In Pittenger's Christology, then, the notion of supernatural grace vanishes. Divine creativity takes its place. One finds oneself left with somewhat less than the Arian Christ, who at least ranked as a super-creature. Pittenger's Jesus, by contrast, confronts one as the best human person God had created so far, one who never allegedly deviated from the subjective aim assigned him by God. How a mere human could accomplish this astonishing feat without succumbing in any way to the corruptions of human society remains unexplained in Pittenger's Christology.[46]

Pittenger, however, reserves all his criticisms for traditional Christian faith instead of focusing them on his own shaky philosophical assumptions. He says not a harsh word about Whitehead's nominalism. Indeed, he endorses enthusiastically Whitehead's flawed, atomized understanding of person and insists that it gives the correct speculative tools for explaining the person of Jesus, who like every other enduring object collapses into a society of overlapping, atomic occasions of experience, a "public matter of fact."[47]

Pittenger's naturalism and neo-Arianism set the pattern for subsequent process Christologies. Like Pittenger, David Griffin prefers Whiteheadean rationalism to neo-orthodox fideism. He concedes to neo-orthodoxy its insistence on revelation but announces that we need to rationalize the notion of divine revelation by identifying natural and special revelation. In other words, Griffin allows one to find God revealed in nature but denies any special, gracious, saving divine intervention in human history that goes beyond the creation of the world.[48]

Besides naturalizing Christian revelation, Griffin also relativizes it. Revelation includes a subjective element. Moreover, everyone views the universe from a different angle. Having equated the historical self-revelation of God with creation, Griffin finds it impossible to endow any finite, historical revelation of God with an absolute character. I find Griffin self-consistent in drawing this conclusion but find no relationship between it and the claims of Christian revelation.[49]

A thorough rationalist, Griffin sees no difference between theology and metaphysics.[50] If Christianity can make any normative claims, it results from the fact that rational reflection on the story of Jesus happens to throw light on the human condition. For reasons he fails to explain, Griffin like Pittenger regards Jesus as sinless. Indeed, Griffin traces the special meaning that Jesus has for us to that gratuitously asserted and unproven fact. Griffin concludes: "Whereas no finality can be claimed for Jesus on the level of the history of ideas, it is possible that his expression of a vision of God, man, the world, and their interrelatedness might be unsurpassable."[51] In other words, they might in fact prove the best that a human being can come up with; on the other hand, they just might not.

Like Pittenger, Griffin holds up Whitehead's philosophy of organism as the norm for Christian belief.[52] Moreover, like Pittenger, he naively assumes the truth and adequacy of Whitehead's philosophy. When one finishes his Christology, one has no sense of the speculative impasses that result from Whitehead's nominalism nor of its failure as a system to interpret ordinary human experience.

John B. Cobb shows more speculative originality in developing his Christology; but he too fails finally to advance beyond unitarianism and a relativized Jesusology. Cobb's originality surfaces in his attempt to reread with Whiteheadean eyes the **Logos** Christology introduced by Justin Martyr and developed by Clement of Alexandria, Origen, and Athanasius.

Cobb assumes that we now live in a post-Christian age that requires a secularized, pluralistic reformulation of Christology. The post-Christian needs to naturalize faith by recognizing that it means the same thing as Heidegger's "authentic existence" and Abraham Maslow's "peak experience."[53] Cobb assumes but fails to demonstrate that "authentic existence" in Heidegger's sense of the term means the same thing as Maslow's "peak experience." One finds other such instances of uncritical, conceptual fuzziness in Cobb's Christological hypothesis.

Cobb echoes basic Whiteheadean theses when he discovers in every occasion of experience openness to unfulfilled potential. He also discovers in each atomic drop of experience an aim to be in a particular way that yields as much satisfaction as circumstances allow. In every atomic moment of experience one discovers a concrete actuality oriented toward a particular unrealized possibility. Cobb calls the experience of unrealized possibility "creativity," although he should, more accurately, have called it reversion. All this rehashes traditional Whiteheadean cosmology.

Cobb, however, makes the process theologian's leap of faith into philosophical rationalism when he identifies "creativity/reversion" with the Christian **"Logos"** and with "Christ." Cobb's "Christ" means the **Logos** conceived as the "order of unrealized potentiality making possible by its immanence the realization of a novel order." In other words, "Christ" means the "cosmic **Logos**" of Platonic and patristic thought reconceived in the light of a Whiteheadean theory of the drive of possibility toward actualization and concreteness.[54]

Having redefined the meaning of "**Logos**" in ways that better accord with Whiteheadean cosmology, Cobb proceeds to develop his Jesusology. He portrays Jesus as a proto-Whiteheadean who called for the unleashing of the creative potential of the **Logos** in the Judaism of his day. Jesus demanded repentance as the condition for such creativity. Moreover, the past fact of Jesus continues to exert a present force on the world which can always enter into the kind of creative relationship with the **Logos** that he announced.

Cobb's Jesus confronts us, moreover, as the supreme incarnation of the creative activity of the "**Logos**" in Cobb's own sense of that term. Like the other process Chistologists we have considered, Cobb insists on the need to replace the traditional understanding of Jesus as a divine person incarnate with a naturalized conception of Jesus as the most creative human person who ever lived. Like Pittenger and Griffin, Cobb offers no justification for regarding Jesus as a privileged revelation of divine creativity; but he promises, implausibly in my opinion, that, if Christians will scrap Chalcedonian faith for Whiteheadean nominalism, they will espouse a theistic faith capable of uniting all the world religions and of inspiring the search for a better social order.[55]

Marjorie Suchocki's ambitious attempt to rethink Christian faith in the light of Whiteheadean cosmology also defends a Whiteheadean unitarianism on the grounds that it offers Christianity a brighter hope than trinitarian faith.

Suchocki suggests that the process vision of an evolving universe offers a philosophical way of reinterpreting what Christian theology has traditionally called "original sin." Suchocki redefines "sin" naturalistically and somewhat narcissistically as closing oneself off to one's own future possibilities.[56] Since, however, in a process universe God and the world relate to one another out of mutual self-interest, in sinning against oneself, as Suchocki suggests, one would also sin indirectly against God by depriving the divine experience of as rich a satisfaction as it might have enjoyed had we acted more creatively.

Suchocki replaces the triune God of Christian faith with the di-polar God of Whiteheadean cosmology. Suchocki's nominalistic cosmology has, however, no more real generality in it than Whitehead's. "Habitual behavior," she remarks, "is simply the convenience of the repetition of activity."[57] In other words, habit boils down to a repetitious series of concrete acts. Like Whitehead's nominalistic deity, Suchocki's has a primordial, consequent, and superject nature. God confronts the world as the creative source of new possibility and as one who seeks maximum concrescence.[58]

Like the other process theologians we have considered so far, Suchocki develops more of a Jesusology than a Christology. She equates creation with incarnation and portrays the goal of the creative process as the full communication of the nature of God to physical creation. "Incarnation" in her theology refers, therefore, not to a unique, personal embodiment of God in a human nature hypostatically united to a divine person, but to any instance of Whiteheadean creativity. Hence, for Suchocki the dynamics of divine incarnation in Jesus differ in no way from the dynamics of creation in any actual entity. Jesus offers the world no supernatural grace or special relationship with God. Instead, "the reality of Jesus, living the love to which he calls the others, enables the others to trust the viability of that kind of living and to dare to create such a world."[59] In other words, Jesus in Suchocki's process universe confronts us as a human person who proclaimed a doctrine of mutual love and who encourages others to live such a doctrine by practicing what he preached.[60] The crucifixion confronts us as the crowning manifestation of love in Jesus' life, which as a moving "incarnation" of God teaches us that "all God's actions are in accordance with love" and that "every pain is felt by God and is therefore God's pain."[61]

Like Pittenger, Griffin, and Cobb, moreover, Suchocki fails finally to explain why anyone should regard the incarnation of God in Jesus as specially revelatory of God; for in the last analysis Suchocki portrays incarnation as co-extensive with creation. This diffusion of the notion of incarnation diffuses its normativity as well. Even if one concedes to Suchocki the human sincerity and self-consistency of Jesus' human life, those traits alone cannot guarantee a divine revelation in Jesus of universal human significance. Nor does her argument justify her suggestion that Jesus gives us a privileged insight into the way God relates to the world.

Having naturalized and diffused the notion of incarnation,

Suchocki also naturalizes and diffuses the notion of resurrection. "Resurrection" in Suchocki's process universe occurs after every particular experience of human suffering, frustration, and defeat. "Resurrection" happens when the God of process integrates a past experience of human pain into his vision of cosmic harmony and offers those who have suffered new possibilities relevant to their histories, possibilities that seek to enhance their further existence in the world by rising above the evil they have suffered.[62]

Things "rise" again, therefore, in the divine primordial nature, which seeks to construct a vision of harmony out of human suffering, defeat, and death. Since things "rise" only insofar as God's vision of cosmic harmony points toward the transcendence of pain, suffering, and evil, the term "resurrection" describes an aspect of the divine process. In a sense, one would do better to speak of God rising above sin, suffering, and defeat rather than of Jesus rising from the dead. "God is not only the power of the resurrection, God is the resurrection."[63] God saves us in Jesus because Jesus reveals God as the power and reality of the resurrection, as the one who constantly seeks to offer the world an alternative to the demonic powers of evil that fragment and destroy it.[64]

In contrast to New Testament theology, the Breath of God plays no role in Suchocki's account of resurrection. Instead, in her naturalistic, rationalistic reading of both incarnation and resurrection, we observe theological Christomonism turning into unitarianism. Suchocki states:

> God as trinity becomes a symbol to indicate the sense in which the unity of God embraces a complexity of magnitude greater than which none can exist. If we thus retain the term trinity to indicate the infinite complexity of the divine nature, we push the word far beyond its traditional meaning of three-ness.[65]

From the standpoint of trinitarian theology what Suchocki calls doctrinal advance sounds more like impoverishment and equivocation. For Suchocki the names "Father," "Son," and "Spirit" designate not divine persons but abstract metaphysical attributes of God. "Father" means the divine power, "Son" means the divine wisdom, and "Spirit" means the divine presence.[66]

While Whiteheadeans have singled out Christology for naturalistic reformulation, we find some concern among them with eschatology as well. Once again, Pittenger sets the pattern.

Pittenger attempts in his eschatology to present the gospel "in starkly human terms." By that Pittenger means that we must not only demythologize the gospel but "unkerygmatize" it as well.[67] "Unkerygmatizing" the gospel means replacing it with Whitehead's philosophy.

Pittenger describes the human experience of death as solitary. While Pittenger regards death as more than a biological fact, he has great doubts about traditional theories of the immortality of the soul. He believes that Christian thinkers have tended in the past to confuse the Greek idea of immortality with the Jewish notion of resurrection of the body. Pittenger's own doctrine of the last things holds out no hope for immortal life after death. When we die, he insists, we die totally: all of us dies. At best we can die having achieved the subjective aim assigned us by God. After death we survive only as a memory in the mind of God. We can, of course, hope for more; but, in the world of Whitehead, we have no assurance that it will happen.[68]

As for divine judgment of the world, Pittenger portrays it as an ongoing process. Judgment means that God makes the best of human decisions as he seeks optimal satisfaction for himself and the living creatures.[69]

Pittenger derides the notion of "heaven" as "pie-in-the-sky-when-you-die." He redefines heaven to mean the enjoyment of God in the present moment. We "rise" only in the sense that God can use our lives in his subsequent quest for divine and cosmic satisfaction. Pittenger applies the same notion of resurrection to Jesus.[70]

In her own eschatology, Marjorie Suchocki attempts to attenuate somewhat the grimness of Pittenger's dekerygmatized vision of the future. While Pittenger rests content with surviving as a memory in the mind of God, Suchocki does not. She attempts to argue on Whiteheadean presuppositions for the possibility of conscious survival in God after death.

She realizes that in order to defend such a position she has to modify Whitehead's philosophy of satisfaction. For Whitehead, satisfaction effects the perishing of immediacy and therefore of all consciousness. Suchocki argues that if satisfaction involves active enjoyment, then it too qualifies as an example of creativity rather than as the mere perishing of immediacy.[71]

Suchocki also argues that actual occasions survive in God with subjective as well as objective immortality; for, if satisfaction includes subjectivity, then in grasping the occasion's satisfaction God feels the subjectivity of the occasion as well as its objectivity. Hence, in God, the occasion attains "its valuation in the immediacy of itself."[72]

Suchocki concludes:

When intensities are understood as the maximal togetherness of embodied eternal objects, the dynamics by which these objects are held together—the subjective experience of the actual occasion—is of paramount importance. Not the remembrance of accomplished intensities but the presentness of experienced intensity is indicated as the continuous aim of God in the creative advance. The subjective immediacy in the everlasting presentness of God would then be the maximum fulfillment of God's purpose. Therefore, we hold that this very subjectivity is everlastingly retained in God's own consequent nature, and that it is this factor which leads Whitehead to the intuition of a final reconciliation of immediacy with objective immortality in everlastingness.[73]

Suchocki argues that only if occasions survive subjectively in God can God overcome the burden of evil that history carries forward. If occasions survive subjectively as well as objectively, then they can through a process of re-evaluation eliminate evil from their satisfactions. If they survive with only objective immortality, then what they experienced as unmitigated evil in this life they will continue to experience everlastingly as unmitigated evil.

In other words, if occasions survive subjectively in God as well as objectively, they can participate in their own redemption; if they survive only objectively, they cannot do so. The redemption of creatures enables God to move successfully to the realization of supreme satisfaction for himself and his creatures, as the universe moves through redemption toward greater and greater harmony.

Suchocki paints an enthusiastic portrait of Whitehead's God as seeking to create a community of communities in which each community knows personal intimacy with itself at the same time that it interrelates with every other community. Moreover, she looks to the dynamic unity of the three natures in God as the ground of cosmic redemption as God gradually lures the universe to the communal union which he desires for it.[74]

At some level, Suchocki senses the inability of Whitehead's nominalistic vision of reality to satisfy the aspirations of Christian hope. When, however, she suggests that one can reconcile her vision of cosmic redemption with Whitehead's system as he formulated it, she lapses, in my opinion, into wishful thinking. Pittenger comes closer to articulating the eschatological consequences of Whitehead's cosmology.

First of all, the atomic character of experience that Whitehead propounds lacks the kind of continuity that would allow satisfaction to include the sort of subjective character that she postulates. Each occasion perishes as it reaches satisfaction, and with its perishing, immediacy perishes as well. Whitehead regarded the perishing of immediacy as a "stubborn fact" and an unavoidable one. He also regarded the perishing of immediacy as the death of each occasion.[75] For Whitehead, the perishing of immediacy means the passage from indeterminacy to total factual definiteness.[76] Creativity functions in the achievement of the definiteness of a satisfaction; but it does not continue to function in the satisfaction itself, which now passes into the objectivity of history.

In order to provide a credible account of the survival of immediacy within satisfaction, Suchocki would have had to subject the nominalistic presuppositions of Whitehead's cosmology to more systematic criticism than she seems willing to undertake. She would in effect have to replace Whitehead's nominalistic, di-polar, atomic account of experience with a triadic, realistic one that endows experience with more real continuity than Whitehead's atomism allows.

As C.S. Peirce saw clearly, if real generality exists and develops with decision, it provides a principle of continuity within development that transcends the atomic drops of experience that Whitehead describes. Real generality, understood as the autonomous habitual tendency to act or to evaluate in specific ways, binds the otherwise discrete moments of human activity into an increasingly complex unity. Since Whitehead's universe lacks real generality, it also lacks the conceptual wherewithal to provide a convincing account of continuity within development. Suchocki would like to think that Whitehead's account of experience allows for the survival of consciousness within satisfaction; but its atomicity combines with its nominalism to rule out such a possibility decisively and in principle.

Without the subjectivity of satisfaction, however, Suchocki's eschatological vision of the divine creation of a community of communities loses its foundation in reality. Moreover, as we have seen, Whitehead's philosophy of relation lacks the conceptual wherewithal to interpret both social experience and the experience of interpersonal relationship. The vision of a community of communities has considerable allure; but it remains unthinkable in the nominalistic world of di-polar theism.

The process theologians we have considered so far have all opted for a method of philosophical reductionism. Instead of dealing with Christian revelation on its own terms, they have opted instead to replace the message of the gospel with concepts derived from Whitehead's philosophical cosmology. Joseph A. Bracken, S.J. counts as a notable exception to this pattern. He recognizes that Catholic theologians will never take Whitehead very seriously unless one can reconcile his cosmological synthesis with Catholic orthodoxy. Accordingly, Bracken develops a process theology thoroughly orthodox in intent.

Bracken concedes the purely hypothetical character of his process theology.[77] Unfortunately, his thought never moves beyond the purely hypothetical into deductive clarification and inductive verification.

Instead of replacing the triune God with the unitarian God of di-polar theism, Bracken states: "To be a person is to belong to a community, i.e., a group of people whose basis for association with one another is their recognition of each other as persons."[78]

Bracken regards the interpersonal community as the highest expression of communal living.[79] He claims to derive his philosophy of community from the thought of A.N. Whitehead and of Josiah Royce. From Whitehead he derives the idea of the interconnectedness of all things; from Royce he derives the notion of interpretation as central to the life of a community.[80]

Unfortunately, however, Bracken fails to deal with the serious philosophical issues that divide Royce from Whitehead. Like Whitehead Royce began his philosophical career espousing a di-polar construct of experience. In **The World and the Individual** he understood human cognitive experience as particular ideas as driving toward concreteness through decision.[81]

C.S. Peirce, on reading **The World and the Individual,** wrote Royce, commending his obvious intelligence, but warning him that he really needed to study logic. Royce took Peirce seriously and as a consequence of studying Peirce's own logic reached what he called his "Peircean insight." Only after he had rejected a di-polar construct of experience and adopted instead Peirce's triadic, realistic construct did Royce develop his philosophy and theology of community. Royce saw more clearly than Bracken does that within a nominalistic epistemology one cannot account for the social aspects of experience or for communal acts of interpretation; for, as we have seen, on Whitehead's nominalistic presuppositions experience takes place entirely within subjectivity. Describing the complex processes of interpretation that structure community life lies beyond the ability of Whitehead's categoreal scheme.

Bracken's philosophical position falls, then, in my opinion, between the two stools of a di-polar nominalism and a triadic realism. Like Schillebeeckx, he wants to talk about the social dimensions of experience without abandoning a fundamentally asocial, di-polar, nominalistic construct of experience. Unlike Royce, he does not seem to recognize the futility of such an attempt.[82]

Bracken portrays the divine persons as each enjoying a "separate" consciousness. Since, however, divine persons have infinite consciousness, they do not view the world from a finite perspective as humans do. They possess a shared consciousness because each knows in its "separate" consciousness identically the same things. Bracken believes that this shared intentionality explains the unity of the Trinity. He argues that the fact that no conflict separates the divine persons rules out a tritheistic interpretation of his construct. He views his position as a development of the traditional trinitarian doctrine of perichoresis, which explains the unity of the trinity as the existence of the divine persons in one another.[83] One may, however, question whether the operational unity of the divine persons that he describes offers finally an adequate account either of perichoresis or of the unity of the Trinity. In my judgment, it does not.

Bracken endorses Whitehead's definition of a person as a monarchically structured society.[84] I find this move unfortunate; for, if one applies such a definition of person to the divine persons, it suggests that in the last analysis each of them fragments into a dubiously unified aggregate of overlapping occasions of experience.[85] Indeed, Bracken describes the divine persons as subsocieties within the divine society, which has the unity of a Whiteheadean structured society.[86]

Bracken, in contrast to the other thinkers we have so far considered, clearly wants to develop a Christology that accords with Chalcedonian orthodoxy; and he succeeds better in this effort than the other process thinkers we have considered. Bracken's doctrine of redemption, however, raises, in my opinion, some important theological questions. Like other process theologians, Bracken uses Whitehead's category of creativity to explain the graced redemption of experience. In making this move he could, in my opinion, appear to blur the distinction between the order of creation and the order of redemption.[87] Similarly, by identifying the initial aim which God assigns to every nexus with actual grace, Bracken would also seem to confuse the process of graced sanctification with creation.[88]

Bracken attempted to explain the philosophical presuppositions of his theological synthesis after he had formulated that synthesis. In **Society and Spirit: A Trinitarian Cosmology**, Bracken faults Ivor Leclerc for assimilating Whitehead's actual occasions to Leibnizian monads exclusively involved in self-constitution.[89]

Bracken offers three arguments in support of this criticism: 1) It goes against the interpretation given Whitehead by most White-headeans. 2) It ignores the superjective character of an occasion of experience. 3) It ignores the collective agency of Whiteheadean societies.[90]

If by Whiteheadeans Bracken means process theologians, I find his appeal to their authority unconvincing, since, as the reader should by now realize, much of process theology consists of an all too often uncritical fusion of Christian and Whiteheadean concepts. In confusing a Whiteheadean society with what ordinary parlance means by social structures, "Whiteheadeans," in my opinion, trade careful textual analysis for wishful thinking. Because they want Whitehead's system to explain Christian experience, they endow his notion of society with meanings Whitehead never intended. By a society, as we have seen, Whitehead meant an enduring object, not social structures in the normal sense of that term. Leclerc, by contrast, remains closer to the text of Whitehead and correctly interprets concrescence as the subjective self-constitution of a drop of experience that defines itself in contrast to the rest of the universe.

Bracken's appeal to the "superjective character" of an occasion of experience in my judgment in no way refutes Leclerc's interpretation of Whitehead. In Whitehead's system an occasion of experience can have superjective influence (i.e. can condition the development of subsequent drops of experience) only after it perishes and is ingested into another atomic instance of experience, whether divine or human. To put the matter in Whiteheadean jargon, the superjective character of an actual entity consists of "the pragmatic value of its specific satisfaction qualifying transcendent creativity."[91] When an entity achieves satisfaction it perishes. It has superjective significance for God and for the experiences that follow it in the society to which it belongs. In other words, what Whitehead means by "superjective influence" does not deny the atomistic, subjective character of experience; on the contrary, "superjective influence" presupposes both.

Finally, Bracken seems to me to undercut his own assertion of the unified agency of a Whiteheadean society when he concedes that Whitehead wanted a society to amount to more than an aggregate but never fully justified that claim.[92] In my opinion, Whitehead's nominalistic, atomistic construct of experience makes the claim unjustifiable in principle. Nor do I find in Bracken's description of a Whiteheadean society as overlapping energy fields of action an adequate account of the unity and continuity of things.[93] To endow experience with unity and continuity, Bracken would, in my opinion, have done better to shift with Royce from a di-polar nominalistic construct of experience to a triadic realistic construct. To make such a shift would, however, demand abandoning Whitehead's system and replacing it with a more adequate one; and that Bracken seems unwilling to do, at least to date.

This chapter has examined the turn to experience in process theology. In it I have argued that among process theologians that turn has to date produced mostly negative theological results. Among Protestant theologians it has yielded a shallow, liberal rationalism that substitutes Whiteheadean cosmology for the Christian gospel. Process rationalism offers many often gratuitous criticisms of Christian orthodoxy; but it makes no serious attempt to criticize the untenable nominalistic philosophical presuppositions of Whitehead's own system. Bracken's effort to formulate an orthodox Christian theology on Whiteheadean presuppositions has, in my judgment, yielded very mixed and largely negative results. Despite the orthodox intent of Bracken's position, it too needs to develop a realistic philosophical foundation if it hopes to do justice to the self-revelation made to us by God in Jesus Christ, in his Holy Breath, and in the church that Breath animates.

In the final chapter of this study, I shall attempt to argue this last point in more detail. Before I do so, however, we need to examine a fourth turn to experience in contemporary theology. I refer to the turn to experience ambitioned by transcendental Thomism.

Notes

[1]Cf. Charles Hartshorne, **The Divine Relativity** (New Haven: Yale University Press, 1948); **Reality as Social Process** (Boston: Beacon,

1953); **The Logic of Perfection and Other Essays** (La Salle: Open Court, 1962); **Anselm's Discovery: A Re-examination of the Ontological Proof for God's Existence** (La Salle: Open Court, 1965); **A Natural Theology for Our Time** (La Salle: Open Court, 1967); **Creative Synthesis and Philosophical Method** (London: SCM Press, 1970). Hartshorne had helped edit the collected papers of C.S. Peirce and therefore knew Peirce's thought. Unfortunately, however, he chose to judge Peirce through Whitehead's nominalistic eyes rather than to judge Whitehead through Peirce's realistic eyes.

[2]Cf. Donald L. Gelpi, S.J., **Experiencing God: A Theology of Human Emergence** (Lanham: University Press of America, 1987).

[3]Alfred North Whitehead, **Process and Reality: Corrected Edition,** edited by David Ray Griffin and Donald W. Sherburne (New York: Free Press, 1978), pp. 15-16.

[4]**Ibid.,** pp. 3-6.

[5]**Ibid.,** p. 9.

[6]**Ibid.,** p. 167.

[7]**Ibid.,** pp. 28-29.

[8]**Ibid.,** pp. 219ff. By a "feeling" Whitehead means a "positive prehension"; by a "positive prehension" he means a concrete fact of relatedness which contributes either physical concreteness or novel possibility to a specific occasion of experience. Every prehension includes three elements: the prehending subject itself, the datum it prehends, and the way it prehends it. **Ibid.,** pp. 22, 23, 26.

[9]**Ibid.,** pp. 219-89.

[10]**Ibid.,** pp. 48-51, 194. When read in the light of Peirce's philosophy, Whitehead's "eternal object" corresponds to Peirce's "quality." Both terms describe not real generality but particular possibility.

[11]**Ibid.,** p. 27.

[12]**Ibid.,** p. 22.

[13]**Ibid.,** p. xiii.

[14]William James, **The Principles of Psychology** (2 vols.; New York: Dover Publications, 1950), vol. 1, pp. 104-05.

[15]William James, **Some Problems of Philosophy: A Beginning of an Introduction to Philosophy** (New York: Longmans Green and Co., 1948), pp. 47-74.

[16]Whitehead, **Process and Reality,** p. 68.

[17]**Ibid.,** pp. 219-80.

[18]**Ibid.,** pp. 22-23.

[19]**Ibid.,** pp. 48-49, 52, 54, 81, 142-43, 152, 158.

[20]**Ibid.**, p. 130.

[21]**Ibid.**, pp. 130-56.

[22]**Ibid.**, p. 113.

[23]**Ibid.**, pp. 20-22.

[24]**Ibid.**, p. 21.

[25]**Ibid.**

[26]Alfred North Whitehead, **Adventures of Ideas** (New York: Mentor, pp. 115-19.

[27]**Ibid.**, pp. 85, 328.

[28]Whitehead, **Process and Reality,** pp.61-82.

[29]**Ibid.**, pp. 29, 60, 82, 223.

[30]**Ibid.**, pp. 71-78.

[31]**Ibid.**, p. 73.

[32]**Ibid.**, pp. 123-26, 310-21.

[33]**Ibid.**, 31-32, 56, 108, 215, 230.

[34]**Ibid.**, p. 198.

[35]**Ibid.**, pp. 26, 342-46.

[36]**Ibid.**, p. 22.

[37]**Ibid.**

[38]Bernard Lee's **The Becoming of the Church** (New York: Paulist, 1974) exemplifies the (in my opinion, illegitimate) tendency of process theologians to read large social structures in the light of a Whiteheadean philosophy of society, or nexus.

[39]**Ibid.**, pp. 351-58.

[40]**Ibid.**, pp. 343-51.

[41]**Ibid.**, p. 88.

[42]**Ibid.**, pp. 26, 160-62.

[43]Whitehead, **Process and Reality,** p. 348.

[44]Cf. Stephen Lee Ely, **The Religious Availability of Whitehead's God** (Madison: University of Wisconsin Press, 1942).

[45]W. Norman Pittenger, **The Word Incarnate: A Study of the Doctrine of the Person of Christ** (London: James Nisbet, 1959) pp. 100-236.

[46]One finds a growing tendency in contemporary theology to equate original sin with social sin. I endorse this tendency and qualify it by suggesting that we must also interpret original sin perspectively. Each person views the universe from a different angle. Each contributes to its total sinfulness. "Original sin" designates to totality of sin in the world minus my personal contribution to it. The sinfulness of the world into which I am born without grace does not, however, lie outside me as an experience. It

enters into experience, shapes it efficaciously, and cozens me into acquiescing in its sinful values. In a word it corrupts me. A person raised in a racist, sexist, classist environment will grow up racist, sexist, and classist. If Jesus was not divine and only human, as Pittenger suggests, then he too would have experienced the corrupting influences of the world and acquiesced in them. Only the efficacious transformation of Jesus' human experience by God could ensure its sinlessness. That, however, would demand that Jesus act with a divine rather than with a human autonomy, even though the same variables that structured us as finite human experiences structured him as well. It would, in a word, demand the hypostatic union. For further discussion of these points, see Donald L. Gelpi, S.J., **Charism and Sacrament: A Theology of Christian Conversion** (New York: Paulist, 1976), pp. 113-31; **Committed Worship: A Sacramental Theology for Converting Christians** (2 vols.; Collegeville: Liturgical Press, 1993), vol. I, chs. 5 & 6; **The Divine Mother: A Trinitarian Theology of the Holy Spirit** (Lanham: University Press of America, 1987), ch. 6.

[47]W. Norman Pittenger, **Christology Reconsidered** (London: SCM Press, 1970).

[48]David R. Griffin, **A Process Christology** (Philadelphia: Westminster, 1973), pp. 9-24. For an alternative view of the relationship between nature and grace, see Donald L. Gelpi, S.J., **Experiencing God: A Theology of Human Emergence** (Lanham: University Press of America, 1987); **Grace as Transmuted Experience and Social Process and Other Essays in North American Theology** (Lanham: University Press of America, 1988).

[49]**Ibid.,** pp. 53-89.

[50]For an alternative approach to method, see Donald L. Gelpi, S.J., **Inculturating North American Theology: An Experiment in Foundational Method** (Atlanta: Scholars Press, 1988).

[51]**Ibid.,** pp. 138-64.

[52]**Ibid.,** pp. 167-92.

[53]John B. Cobb, **Christ in a Pluralistic Age** (Philadelphia: Westminster, 1975), pp. 49-61.

[54]**Ibid.,** pp. 62-95.

[55]**Ibid.,** pp. 97-258.

[56]Marjorie Hewett Suchocki, **God, Christ, Church: A Practical Guide to Process Theology** (New York: Crossroad, 1982), p. 28.

[57]**Ibid.,** p. 53.

[58]**Ibid.,** pp. 38-66.

[59]**Ibid.**, p. 102.

[60]**Ibid.**, pp. 93-102.

[61]**Ibid.**, pp. 102-09.

[62]**Ibid.**, pp. 111-15.

[63]**Ibid.**, p. 115.

[64]**Ibid.**, pp. 115-17.

[65]**Ibid.**, p. 215.

[66]**Ibid.**, pp. 213-23.

[67]W. Norman Pittenger, **"The Last Things" in a Process Perspective** (London: Epworth, 1970), pp. 24-25.

[68]**Ibid.**, pp. 30-41, 84-85.

[69]**Ibid.**, pp. 46-60.

[70]**Ibid.**, pp. 62-99.

[71]Marjorie Hewett Suchocki, **The End of Evil: Process Eschatology in Historical Context** (Albany: State University of New York Press, 1988), pp. 85-89.

[72]**Ibid.**, pp. 90-93.

[73]**Ibid.**, p. 94.

[74]**Ibid.**, pp. 115-52.

[75]Whitehead, **Process and Reality,** pp. xiii-xiv.

[76]**Ibid.**, pp. 29, 212.

[77]Joseph A. Bracken, S.J., **The Triune Symbol: Persons, Process, and Community** (Lanham: University Press of America, 1985), pp. 3-4.

[78]**Ibid.**, p. 17.

[79]**Ibid.**, pp. 16-17.

[80]**Ibid.**, pp. 19-22.

[81]Josiah Royce, **The World and the Individual: First Series** (New York: Dover, 1959) pp. 265-382.

[82]Bracken discusses the positions of Whitehead and Royce in "Authentic Subjectivity and Genuine Objectivity," **Horizons** (Fall, 1984), vol. 11, no. 2, pp. 290-303. In my judgment, however, he underestimates the subtlety and complexity of Royce's thought in comparison with Whitehead's. The mature Royce developed a metaphysics as complex as Whitehead's and, in my estimation, subtler and truer to the social dimensions of human experience. (See Frank M. Oppenheim, **Royce's Mature Philosophy of Religion** (Notre Dame: Notre Dame University Press, 1987). Bracken fails to explain in ways that makes sense to me how one would reconcile Royce's and Whitehead's understanding of society.

[83]**Ibid.**, pp. 24-26. For an alternative account of the unity of the Trinity

using a triadic construct of experience, see Gelpi, **The Divine Mother,** ch. 6.

[84]**Ibid.,** p. 24.

[85]**Ibid.,** pp. 39-43.

[86]**Ibid.,** pp. 44-45.

[87]**Ibid.,** pp. 86-96.

[88]**Ibid.,** pp. 111-81.

[89]Joseph A. Bracken, S.J., **Society and Spirit: A Trinitarian Cosmology** (London: Associated University Presses, 1991), p. 41.

[90]**Ibid.,** pp. 41-44.

[91]Whitehead, **Process and Reality,** p. 87.

[92]**Ibid.,** p. 43.

[93]**Ibid.,** pp. 51ff.

4

The Turn to Experience in Transcendental Thomism

As I have already suggested, among transcendental Thomists Bernard Lonergan made the turn to experience when he suggested that a strictly normative account of the experience of conversion grounds the work of theological reconstruction. Lonergan also called for a systematic multi-disciplinary exploration of diverse kinds of conversion experience.[1] Among contemporary transcendental Thomists, however, Karl Rahner in his own way also attempted something like a turn to experience. He did so in his reflections on human consciousness of a transcendental orientation toward mystery.[2]

In my own judgment, Lonergan has succeeded better in making the turn to experience than Rahner did. Two elements in Rahner's thought principally conspired to subvert the turn he attempted. First, he acquiesced in an indefensible Kantian logic. Second, he fallaciously presupposed that one can use such a logic to formulate a metaphysics in the classical sense of that term. By classical metaphysics I mean an account of reality that claims to reach a universal, necessary insight into Being.[3] As we shall see, both of these presuppositions led Rahner to approach human experience prescriptively rather than to deal with experience on its own terms.

Rahner learned these misleading presuppositions from Joseph Maréchal, who laid the philosophical foundations for transcendental Thomism. The same assumptions also function to some extent in Lonergan's early thought, although the Lonergan of **Method in Theology** has in part begun to transcend them. As we shall see, however, Lonergan never fully escaped the fallacies of Kantianism or of Thomism. To the end he defended an inadequate notion of experience patterned on Kant's concept of a sense manifold and colored by Thomistic intellectualism.

In evaluating Lonergan's concept of experience, I shall argue that Lonergan's theory of theological method forces the revision of his understanding of experience. In describing the work of foundational theology, Lonergan calls for a systematic, multi-disciplinary investigation of conversion in all its forms. In this chapter and in the one that follows, I shall argue that such an investigation demonstrates the inadequacy of Lonergan's philosophical understanding of experience and demands its revision.

Both Lonergan and Rahner, however, did manage to avoid the nominalism that plagues the three turns to experience that the three preceding chapters have already examined. Lonergan explicitly defended the reality of laws in nature as well as the mind's ability to grasp them.[4] Rahner, like a true Aristotelian, believed in the reality of fixed and immutable substantial essences that endow created powers of operation with fixed dynamic tendencies toward fixed formal objects.[5] As a consequence, Rahner the philosopher lived in the relatively static, hierarchical universe of classical metaphysics. That metaphysics recognized the reality of generality, although it tended to conceive it as essentially fixed. In addition, however, Rahner the theologian also recognized the evolution of the laws of nature as a plausible scientific hypothesis, although he never undertook to explain how one might go about reconciling that hypothesis with the world of fixed and unchanging essences that his own metaphysics propounded.[6]

In this chapter I shall reflect on these issues in greater detail. My argument divides into three parts. First, I shall examine the work of Joseph Maréchal who laid systematic philosophical foundations for transcendental Thomism by blending Kantian logic and epistemology with Thomistic metaphysics. His work colors profoundly the attempts of both Rahner and Lonergan to make the turn to experience. Second, I shall show that Rahner's acquiescence in the fallacies of Maréchal's philosophy explains why his phenomenological turn to experience abandoned description for prescription. Third, I shall examine the turn to experience in Lonergan's mature thought. I shall argue that Lonergan defends an inadequate philosophical understanding of the term "experience."

(I)

In order to appreciate both the glories and the woes of Marechalian Thomism, one must situate Maréchal in his era. Maréchal, like Rahner, Lonergan, and all pre-Vatican-II speculative theologians, worked in the shadow of **Aeterni Patris**. This encyclical of Leo XIII, issued in 1879, established Thomism as a norm for philosophical orthodoxy among Catholic thinkers.[7] After **Aeterni Patris** all Catholic philosophers had to speculate **en bon Thomist** or risk the wrath of the holy office. Those who wanted to develop a Thomism relevant to contemporary times had, as a consequence, to blend Thomistic insights with others derived from more contemporary thinkers. This state of affairs persisted until the Second Vatican Council.

Maréchal also wrote at a difficult time for Catholic intellectuals. The modernist controversy was just subsiding. Witch-hunting for modernist heretics had ceased, but cautious integralists kept their weather-eyes cocked for signs of modernist deviance among Catholic intellectuals. Moreover, the latter had to submit everything they wrote to antecedent ecclesiastical censorship.

Between 1922 and 1923 Maréchal issued the first three volumes of his monumental philosophical study, **Le point de depart de la metaphysique** (The Starting Point of Metaphysics). In it he attempted to reply to Kant's claim that he, Kant, had buried metaphysics for good and had reduced the idea of God to an empty, unverifiable concept. As the title of Maréchal's work indicates, at one level it ambitioned a thoroughly conservative goal, the rehabilitation of Aquinas' creative reformulation of classical Aristotelian metaphysics; but Maréchal did so in speculatively innovative ways.

Maréchal had devised a daring plan for refuting Kantianism. He intended to put Thomism into dialogue with Kantian transcendental philosophy. By doing so, Maréchal believed that he could refute Kant on Kant's own presuppositions. Maréchal therefore adopted the "turn to the subject" that characterizes transcendental philosophy. In the process, he also implicitly endorsed the presuppositions of Kantian logic.

As we have already seen, Kantian logic fails to distinguish clearly between hypothetical, deductive, and inductive inference. Instead, Kantian logic looks on all inference as deductive. As a consequence, anyone using Kantian logic argues by formulating an unproven hypothesis which one then presents as a validated, inductive inference at the same time that one calls the unproven hypothesis a transcendental deduction.

Maréchal not only tacitly endorsed these confused, Kantian logical presuppositions, he also put them to much more ambitious use than ever Kant had. Kant had argued that transcendental logic provides a useful method for exploring the structure of human subjectivity but that it can never yield a metaphysical insight into the real. Maréchal, however, wanted to use this flawed logic in order to revalidate classical metaphysics by grounding it in a Thomistic analysis of human subjectivity.

After the publication of the first three volumes of **Le point de depart,** Maréchal found himself under heavy integralist attack for having espoused Kantianism. In 1920 the works of Kant still languished on the Index of Forbidden Books, which no Catholic could read without episcopal permission. To integralist eyes, Maréchal, in cozying up to Kant, seemed to be fraternizing with the enemy.

In order to defend himself from this attack Maréchal published the fifth volume of his projected study before publishing the fourth. In the first four volumes, he had intended to deal with historical considerations, issues in the development of philosophy; only the fifth volume gave systematic articulation to Maréchal's own position. As things turned out, the fourth volume would not appear in print until after Maréchal's death in 1944.

In the fifth and final volume, Maréchal argued that a Thomistic theory of knowledge anticipates all the issues raised by Kant and offers a better analysis of human subjectivity than Kant himself. Maréchal argued correctly that Kant's attempt to do in metaphysics rested on a simplistic, di-polar construct of human understanding. As we have seen, Kant acquiesced in the nominalistic construct of cognition popularized by British empiricism. Kant therefore understood cognition as the subjective interrelation of percepts and concepts. In the process, Maréchal argued, Kant had overlooked that very aspect of human knowing that formed the centerpiece of Aquinas' theory of knowledge: namely, the intellectual judgment of being. Aquinas realized more clearly than Kant had, Maréchal argued, that we interrelate percepts and concepts cognitively in order to form judgments about the things we know with our senses. When we make true judgments, then, we grasp more than the relationship between percepts and concepts: in fact, we grasp the being, the reality of the things we know.

Here three points need emphasizing. First, in Maréchalean Thomism one encounters a fusion of Kantian and Thomistic theory of knowledge. For Maréchal as for Aquinas, the lower powers of knowing—the external and internal senses—provide the raw materials of judgment. They therefore function much as the "sense manifold" does in Kant: namely, they provide the matter of thought that the intellect conceptualizes and judges. In making a judgment, however, the Thomistic intellect does more than categorize sense data in the manner of the Kantian intellect; for the Thomistic intellect grasps sensible objects as being and not just as sensible.

Second, in its understanding of human cognition, Maréchalean Thomism acquiesces in the extreme intellectualism of Thomistic theory of knowledge. Only the privileged spiritual faculties of intellect and will can grasp being as such. The intellect does it cognitively, the will does it decisively. The sense powers reveal real things to us but do not grasp them as real, only as colored, smelly, tasty, etc.

Third, Maréchal had no difficulty in documenting the contrast between a Thomistic and a Kantian theory of knowledge. When, however, he argued that he could use Kantian transcendental logic in order to reground classical metaphysics in a Thomistic theory of knowledge, he enunciated a massive philosophical **non sequitur**.

Maréchal argued that the fact that the intellect makes judgments of being proves that Being functions as the formal object of the intellect and establishes the truth of a Thomistic doctrine of the powers and nature of the soul. In so arguing, he assumed the truth of the Thomistic psychology that he asserted, but without ever proving it. As we have seen, however, Kantian logic sanctions such a **non sequitur** by confusing hypothesis with demonstration.

Had Maréchal distinguished clearly between hypothetical, deductive, and inductive thinking, he would have recognized the fallibility of any and all hypotheses, and especially of world-hypotheses. A world-hypothesis offers an interpretation of the nature of reality in general. It aspires to universality, but it can claim no **a priori** necessity. Moreover, a single exception to its generalizations calls such an hypothesis into question.

Classical metaphysics, as we have seen, fallaciously regards its hypotheses not only as universal but as necessarily true. Maréchal fallaciously thought that he could use Kantian transcendental logic to reground such a metaphysics. In other words, he fallaciously assumed that the mere assertion of the truth of Thomistic faculty psychology and of Thomistic metaphysics established its universal truth, necessarily and **a priori.**

With the mature Lonergan, I would hold that one need not and, indeed, should not explain the human ability to make judgments by appealing to Thomistic faculty psychology.[8] I shall argue this point in greater detail below. Here it suffices to note that, for Maréchal, writing as he did in the 1920s, no other psychology qualified as orthodox. Maréchal, however, wanted earnestly to establish his Thomistic orthodoxy against the slanders of his critics. Moreover, at the time, liberal Catholic intellectuals applauded Maréchal for having successfully used Kant to update Thomism and prove its contemporary relevance. It did not occur to either Maréchal or to his supporters to submit either Kantian logic or Thomistic theory of knowledge to the kind of radical critique that they brought against Kantian epistemology. Nor did it occur to them to question Thomistic faculty psychology in the light of empirical investigations of the human psyche. Instead, Kantian logic combined with the claims of classical metaphysics to betray them into assuming that their privileged metaphysical insight into the necessary and universal structure of the human spirit had "grounded" philosophically any results that mere empirical investigation of the human psyche might suggest.

In other words, the political situation of the church conspired with the confusions of Kantian logic to betray Maréchal and his followers into confusing the enunciation of an epistemological hypothesis with its validation. It would take five decades before Jean Piaget would pop this particular bubble of philosophical illusion by calling quite correctly for the multi-disciplinary validation of philosophical theories of knowledge through the empirical techniques like those he employed in his development psychology.[9]

In the meantime, the illusions that Maréchal popularized would have profound effect on the development of transcendental Thomism. Both Lonergan and Rahner began their intellectual careers in the same intellectually repressive atmosphere as Maréchal. Both regarded Maréchal's thought as philosophically **avant garde.** Both acquiesced in its oversights and fallacies.

In his attempt to reground Thomistic metaphysics in Kantian logic and Thomistic epistemology, Maréchal painted an inflated portrait of human intellectual curiosity. He described the Thomistic intellect as a dynamic appetite for Being. The fact that Being functions as the formal object of the human intellect endows the latter with a virtual (or negative) infinity. Finite itself, the spiritual intellect longs insatiably for more and more being. This longing manifests itself in the restless, never ending human search for truth; for in Thomistic metaphysics truth and Being coincide.

For Marechal the necessary, universal, **a priori** structure of the human spirit explains this intellectual restlessness. The formal object of the intellect orients it to Being as such. Because in any given judgment the intellect grasps, not Being as such, but this particular being, no finite object of judgment exhausts the intellect's longing for truth. Only the union of the intellect with subsistent Being, with God, can satisfy that longing.

Maréchal drew two important conclusions from these assumptions about the workings of the human mind. First, he argued that because the formal object of the intellect orients it to God, every time the intellect says "is," it implicitly says "God." In other words, the **a priori** structure of the human spirit not only proves its ability to grasp finite created being but also demonstrates its essential, necessary orientation to uncreated, infinite Being, namely, to God. Second, because perfect union with God occurs only in the beatific vision, Marechal, together with Thomas Aquinas, discovered in the natural dynamism of the spiritual intellect toward Being as such a "natural desire for the beatific vision."[10]

I have reflected elsewhere on the confusions that transcendental Thomism has introduced into a contemporary understanding of the relationship between nature and grace. Here I focus on the ways it has skewed the attempts of both Rahner and Lonergan to make the turn to experience, although the present discussion will have to confront some of the same issues.

(II)

In **Spirit in the World** and in **Hearers of the Word,** Karl Rahner espouses and attempts to develop the insights of Marechalean Thomism. Rahner not only endorses Maréchal's philosophical use of Kantian logic; he finds in it the key to theological thinking as well. Indeed, Kantian logic provides Rahner with the fundamental question his theology attempts to explore: namely, what are the conditions for the possibility of the divine revelation we have received in Jesus Christ?

The same epistemological presuppositions that ground Rahner's early work also function in his mature thought. In **Foundations of Christian Faith,** Rahner distinguishes both an **a priori** and an **a posteriori** dimension in the human experience of God. Our experience of God has an **a posteriori** dimension because it occurs only in the course of our experience of the world around us. In the course of our interaction with the world, however, we become aware of the **a priori** orientation of the human spirit to God. This orientation expresses the necessary, universal essence of Spirit. It exists only unconsciously and unthematically until we thematize it through concepts derived from our interaction with the world.[11]

When most people hear Rahner talking about the unconscious, transcendental structures of the human spirit, I suspect that they imagine that he is talking about the Freudian unconscious, or at least about some variation of it. In point of fact, he is talking about nothing of the sort. Rather, he is talking Thomistic faculty psychology.

In Thomistic anthropology no one ever experiences as such either a substance or the powers of activity that mysteriously emanate from it.[12] Rather one infers their existence from the activities of things. The substance and its powers of activity undergird activity. The acts that flow from those powers, however, manifest the powers' dynamic orientation and allegedly reveal their formal object.

In speaking of an unconscious, unthematic dynamism in the human spirit, Rahner is really talking primarily about the active and passive intellects. He regards both of these powers as purely spiritual.[13] Their unconscious character has, therefore, absolutely nothing to do with the Freudian unconscious, which in Thomistic psychology would engage the lower powers of the sensible soul: namely, the memorative, the imaginative, the irascible, and the conscupiscible powers.[14] No, the unconscious dynamism of which Rahner is speaking has a purely spiritual, completely disembodied character.

The unconscious dynamism of spirit of which Rahner speaks roots itself finally in the formal object of the spiritual agent intellect. When the active spiritual intellect moves the passive spiritual intellect to make judgments, the latter grasps sensible reality as being. On Thomistic presuppositions, the act of judging therefore reveals that both active and passive intellectual powers have Being as such as their formal objects. The active intellect, however, thrusts toward Being actively. It therefore represents for Rahner a dynamic, pre-apprehension (**Vorgriff**) of Being. The judgmental grasp of sensible realities allegedly raises this **Vorgriff** to consciousness.[15]

Since together with Maréchal, Rahner assumes uncritically the truth not only of Thomistic faculty psychology but of Thomistic metaphysics as well, he also equates Being, the formal object of the active and passive intellects, with the infinite Being of God.[16] Among transcendental Thomists Joseph Maréchal and Henri de Lubac both endorse the Thomistic idea that the spiritual intellect's dynamic thirst for Being expresses a natural desire for the beatific vision. Rahner, by contrast, deems that a natural desire for a supernatural reality sounds too much like Pelagianism.

Rahner therefore argues, again on purely **a priori** grounds, that if the human spirit experiences a desire for the beatific vision, that desire must result from grace, not from the nature of the intellect alone. He therefore postulates his famous supernatural existential. He proposes that God has expanded the natural orientation of the human spirit to himself into an **a priori** supernatural desire to know the triune God revealed to us in Jesus Christ.[17]

I cut my theological teeth on Rahner;[18] and for a number of years I defended his theory of the supernatural existential. I did so until my encounters with converts to Christianity from secular unbelief convinced me that Rahner's theory does not in fact interpret such an experience of conversion.

Rahner rarely mentions conversion. The idea does not function significantly in his theological synthesis. Conversion describes a graced transformation of human experience. Rahner's theory of the supernatural existential demands, however, that one hold that, as soon as a human spirit comes into existence in the womb, it has built into it **a priori**, with both necessity and universality, a graced, supernatural longing not only for God but for Christ.[19] As a consequence, when Rahnerian converts pass from unbelief to faith they simply recognize explicitly and thematically what they have always been all along: viz. an "anonymous Christian," a spiritual, graced longing for Christ. In converting, they merely thematize the **a priori**, supernatural longing for Christ that God somehow (Rahner never explains how) built into their spirits in creating them.[20]

Unfortunately, for my naive faith in the theory of the supernatural existential, the converts from unbelief to belief with whom I dealt pastorally found Rahner's theory so much unintelligible, academic jargon. It did not interpret for them at all their experience of coming to faith. Instead of talking about thematizing their **a priori** orientation to Christ, they gravitated more to the language of the New Testament. They described the transforming consequences of Christian conversion in the power of the Spirit more as their rebirth or as their re-creation. Conversion from unbelief to belief in an incarnate God had not revealed to them what they had always been. Instead, it had effected a sea change in their lives. It had transformed them into radically different kinds of persons.

Encounters with such converts shook my faith in the supernatural existential but did not entirely destroy it. Eventually, however, my study of Peirce's logic combined with the contradictions present in Thomistic faculty psychology to convince me of the theoretical indefensibility of Rahner's theory. Peirce's critique of Kantian logic convinced me that the mere enunciation of a theory of the supernatural existential proves nothing about its truth.

Moreover, once one understands the theory's presuppositions, one realizes that its truth stands or falls with Thomistic faculty psychology, which it tacitly presupposes; for Rahner has conceived the supernatural existential precisely as a way of avoiding what he considers the Pelagian implications of the Thomistic notion of a natural desire for the beatific vision. That desire expresses the agent intellect's **Vorgriff** of Being.

In other words, unless one can establish the truth of Thomistic faculty psychology, one has no grounds for asserting the supernatural existential. Moreover, justifying faculty psychology forces one to justify as well the world of classical Greek metaphysics that it presupposes. Unfortunately, however, that world builds on the essence fallacy.

One who commits the essence fallacy illegitimately reifies essences. In constructing their philosophies both Plato and Aristotle invoked the essence fallacy. Plato reified essences as transcendent, subsistent ideas. Aristotle reified them as unchanging principles of being immanent within things.

The empirical evidence supporting evolutionary theory seems to me to call seriously into question a classical philosophy of essence. The classical Greek philosophers imagined reality as a great chain of being: as fixed and hierarchically organized essences of greater or less perfection. This static, hierarchical view of reality reflected in many ways the static, hierarchical societies that prevailed both in Greco-Roman times and during the middle ages.

In an evolving universe essences exist but neither as subsistent realities nor as metaphysical principles of being. Rather, the term "essence" designates a human evaluative response—a sensation, image, or conceptual perception—abstracted from the reality it perceives and from the one who does the perceiving. In an evolving universe, the dynamisms present in things result from their evolving histories, not from some fixed, unchanging essence lurking within them.

In other words, in an evolving universe more than the powers of the soul evolve; every emerging self also evolves. What a thing is results, not from some fixed essence lurking underneath its activity, but from its history. Each emerging self embodies a developing, more or less integrated complex of tendencies. In an evolving universe, therefore, one can no longer speak of fixed substantial essences giving rise with necessity and universality to powers of activity endowed with fixed formal objects. Rather, once one recognizes the illegitimacy of the essence fallacy and acknowledges the evolving, developmental character of reality, the classical philosophical presuppositions on which faculty psychology constructs its theory of knowledge collapse; and with their collapse Maréchalean Thomism comes tumbling down as well.[21]

Study of the developmental psychology of Jean Piaget further convinced me that Maréchal's portrayal of the human intellect as an insatiable appetite for truth has finally no basis in fact. Close empirical investigation of the way human minds develop reveals, not their virtual infinity, but their radical finitude. For two years the human mind cannot even imagine a world. The infant lives in a world of sensations, emotions, and concrete memories. The ability to imagine a world does not surface until about the age of two. Children do not learn to reason until years later; and, when they do, they construct very finite frames of reference for dealing with the world, frames of reference whose inadequacy dooms them to eventual collapse. In other words, Piaget's developmental psychology seemed to me to lend empirical support to belief in the radical fallibility and finitude of the human mind of which American philosophers speak.[22]

My studies in clinical psychology also confirmed me in the belief that ego-inertia rather than insatiable curiosity better describes the way that human minds develop. As a teacher, I kept looking for students with the kind of "unrestricted desire to know" that Maréchal says they not only should but must have. I never found a single one. On the contrary, I found minds threatened by novel insight as soon as novelty requires the willingness to criticize familiar presuppositions.

My study of philosophy, theology, and psychology also dramatized for me that even the most brilliant minds suffer from gaps, omissions, and oversights that they show little desire to overcome. My experiences in the groves of academia gave me even less reason for believing in the unrestricted desire to know. The massive egos that one so often encounters among academics all too frequently display massive obtuseness to the opinions and insights of others. IQ tests and similar empirical measurement of human cognitive ability provided still more empirical evidence that the virtually infinite intellects of which transcendental Thomists speak simply do not exist.

Finally, the logical contradictions inherent in Thomistic faculty psychology also led me to part company with it definitively. At the heart of Thomistic faculty psychology lies an operational dualism. Aquinas divided the powers of the soul into sensible organic powers and spiritual powers. The sense powers include the five external senses, sensible memory and imagination, as well as the concupiscible and irascible appetites. The active and passive intellects as well as the will qualify as spiritual and therefore lack any organic basis.

Unfortunately, if one accepts such an account of the human psyche, one cannot explain how intellectual knowledge arises from the senses, even though it obviously does. In faculty psychology, the formal object of a power of the soul both defines and restricts the scope of its activity. As a consequence, powers restricted by their formal objects to deal with sensible, material things as sensible have no ability to affect spiritual realities, which exist on a higher rung in the ladder of metaphysical perfection. The essential, ontological superiority of the spiritual powers of the soul to the world of sense places both the spiritual intellect and the spiritual will beyond the reach of sensible activity.

Aquinas defended such an operational dualism but nevertheless affirmed with Aristotle the sensible origin of all intellectual
knowledge. The angelic doctor, with his usual insight, recognized
the difficulty inherent in holding both positions simultaneously. He
tried to explain the sensible origin of intellectual knowledge by
arguing that the agent intellect uses the phantasm in the sensible
imagination to impress an idea on the passive intellect, much as a
pencil held in a human hand can write not just physical marks but
meaningful words on a page. His analogy limped, of course. The
agent intellect has to use the sensible phantasm in the imagination
to "write" not on a page but on the spiritual, passive intellect.
Aquinas might as well have talked about one Thomistic angel
using a slide projector to project not an image but an idea onto
another Thomistic angel.

In Peirce's phenomenology and metaphysics of experience,
by contrast, one can describe both spatio-temporal realities and
realities that transcend space and time without appealing to the
classical Greek categories of "spirit" and "matter."[23] As I pondered,
moreover, the havoc and confusion that spirit-matter dualism had
wrought upon the Christian mind and upon Christian spirituality I
waved goodbye to spirit-matter language with never a tear.

Let me, then, sum up these reflections on Rahner's anthropology and theology of grace. The more I pondered the philosophical
presuppositions that lend plausibility to Rahner's theory of the
supernatural existential, the more I saw that the theory rests on an
inadequate logic, on a false and inflated belief in the virtual infinity
of the human mind, and on a contradictory and unverifiable
account of human cognition.

Why, then, does Rahner's theology enjoy such popularity
among contemporary Catholics? Ego-inertia provides a partial
explanation. A theological community habituated for over a century to thinking almost exclusively in Thomistic patterns of thought
seems to find it virtually impossible to shift to more inculturated
patterns of philosophical reflection. Ego-inertia alone, however,
does not explain everything.

The more I pondered this question the more I began to suspect that, in a strange, paradoxical way, Rahner's turn to experi-

ence motivates his popularity. His turn to experience appeals for its plausibility to two fundamental human experiences. It appeals explicitly to the common human experience of mystery; and it appeals implicitly to the adult conversion experience of cradle Christians. Let me explain what I mean.

Every human mind, of course, experiences mystery. Unfortunately, however, Rahner's anthropology offers a false and unverifiable explanation of why humans experience mystery. Rahner believes that faculty psychology and the formal object of the agent intellect, its **a priori Vorgriff** of Being, explain the human experience of mystery. That **Vorgriff,** which endows the human intellect with a negative infinity, gives the agent intellect an unconscious, natural desire for Being and for God. Moreover, God has somehow mysteriously and graciously transformed this natural desire for Being into an unthematic, graced desire for Christ and the beatific vision.

In my judgment, Rahner's explanation of the experience of mystery has it exactly backward. The finitude of the human mind, not its virtual infinity, explains the all too common human experience of mystery. The world, life, reality seem mysterious to us when we run out of explanations for why things happen the way they do. Moreover, given our finite angle on the world and limited insight into reality, in dealing with events of any magnitude and complexity, we usually run out of plausible explanations relatively fast. When that happens, we find ourselves thrown back on vague, intuitive hunches and guesses or on sheer bewilderment. When our bewilderment reaches awesome proportions, we experience mystery. By the same token, we experience the encounter with God as mysterious because the supreme, all-encompassing perfection of the divine experience means that it always eludes comprehensive conceptualization and explanation by finite, peanut brains like ourselves.

In other words, in describing the encounter with God in faith as mysterious, Rahner appeals to a common human experience that makes his theology popularly appealing as long as one refuses to look too closely at his flawed and unverifiable explanation of that experience. Moreover, on the basis of endless discussion about

Rahner with colleagues and students, I am inclined to believe that most students of Rahner rest content with having scratched some semblance of experiential meaning from his rambling, arcane, and convoluted prose. Relatively few bother to probe beyond his theological assertions to the flawed philosophical presuppositions that ground them. Fewer still subject those presuppositions to the kind of radical criticism that they badly need.

Similarly, I find it entirely understandable when cradle Christians resonate with Rahner's theory of the supernatural existential. In some ways, the idea of unthematized grace waiting for thematization by an adult act of faith interprets the adult conversion experience of those raised in an atmosphere of faith. Allow me to explain what I mean.

I noted above that the converts from unbelief to belief with whom I dealt pastorally could make little sense of Rahner's theology of unthematic grace. It makes more sense to cradle Christians, however, because cradle Christians convert differently than unbelievers. Unbelievers pass from no faith to faith; cradle Christians pass from infantile faith to childish faith to adolescent faith and then, hopefully, to adult faith. When, therefore, cradle Christians come to a responsible, autonomous, adult religious faith—when, in other words, they convert as adult Christians—they often find that the language of unthematic grace interprets their experience. In taking responsibility for their personal response to God, they seem to be making explicit and conscious a less thematic faith that they have had all along.

Once again, however, Rahner points to a real human experience but gives it the wrong explanation. If Rahner has the right of it, then the logic of his position demands that these same people have had an implicit, unthematized longing for Christ even in their mothers' wombs. They do so because God, who has created and saved the world by using transcendental, Kantian logic, has built that longing into their spirits with **a priori** necessity.

I suspect that Germans find it easier than most to believe in a God who thinks with Kantian logic. I, however, find it unlikely that God in creating the universe would have used a logic whose inadequacy even finite human minds can grasp. I therefore also doubt that, when cradle Christians convert, they thematize a faith built into their psyches from the moment of their conception. When cradle Christians convert as adults, they simply make explicit and thematic a relationship to God that they have acquired in the course of their religious education. When non-Christians or unbelievers convert to Christianity they have a very different kind of experience.

Unfortunately, however, Rahner's theory of the supernatural existential demands that unbelievers and non-Christians have the same conversion kind of experience as cradle Christians. For Rahner, atheists, agnostics, and non-Christian religionists all count as "anonymous Christians." In other words, Rahner's **a priori** logic combines with his indefensible assumption that it grasps the necessary, universal structure of the human spirit in order to prevent him from adequately dealing with religious experience on its own terms, especially with the variety and complexity of non-Christian, religious experience.

Rahner's philosophical assumptions demand that he interpret all religious experience prescriptively, that he legislate with **a priori** universality and necessity how it has to develop. A human spirit with a supernatural existential has to experience reality implicitly in the same way that a Christian does because the theory of the supernatural existential prescribes only one possible explanation of the human experience of mystery. That experience must result from the **a priori** gracing of the formal object of the agent intellect. The idea that all non-Christians are implicitly Christian may give comfort to some in a secularized world. In my judgment, however, the conversion experiences of unbelievers point in a different direction and call for a different understanding of the relationship between nature and grace than Rahner has articulated.[24]

In the end, therefore, Rahner's prescriptive approach to human religious experience blinds him to its actual variety and leaves him bereft of categories to deal adequately with the plurality of faiths and of conversion experiences. In other words, Rahner's turn to experience fails finally, in my judgment, because an inadequate logic, anthropology, and metaphysics force him to misinterpret the significance of the very experiences to which his theology turns. Instead of dealing with the varieties of religious experiences on their own terms, Rahner demands that experience conform to the Procrustian bed of his own questionable philosophical and theological assumptions.

(III)

The mature Lonergan also makes the turn to experience; but he seems to me to have escaped many of the fallacies that trouble the turn that Rahner attempted. As we have seen, unlike Rahner, the mature Lonergan rejects Thomistic faculty psychology. In addition, he has replaced the metaphysical approach to God which he developed in **Insight** with strictly normative reflection on the experience of conversion itself. Moreover, instead of attempting to explain conversion exclusively in terms of a dated metaphysical anthropology, as Rahner does, Lonergan, having abandoned faculty psychology, calls for an interdisciplinary investigation that respects the pluralism of human thought and experience.[25]

In other words, Lonergan's turn to experience seems to respect more than Rahner's does the complexity and variety of human experience, whether religious or secular. With Piaget, Lonergan recognizes that in a contemporary context any theology of experience must take into explicit account both empirical investigations of conversion and empirical explorations of human experience in general. Lonergan also recognizes the legitimacy of approaching experience in a variety of conceptual frames of reference.

In addition, Lonergan recognizes better than Rahner does variety and complexity within conversion. Lonergan has, for example, challenged theologians to recognize that conversion happens in secular as well as in religious contexts.[26] Before Lonergan made his suggestion, theologians had traditionally conceived conversion as an essentially religious event with moral and social consequences. Traditionally, one converts from sin and unbelief to the obedience of Christian faith. Moreover, that conversion inserts one into a worshiping Christian community of faith. Hence, the rites of sacramental initiation seal and complete the experience of conversion.

Lonergan's theology of conversion in no way denies these traditional insights into the dynamics of Christian conversion; but it insists that conversion can and does occur in other than religious contexts. Initially, Lonergan spoke of two other kinds of conversion: moral and intellectual. He later conceded a third kind: namely, affective conversion.

In sum, then, among transcendental Thomists Lonergan's turn to experience advances significantly beyond Rahner's in its respect for empirical investigations into human religious experience, in its overt conceptual pluralism, and in its recognition of both secular and religious forms of conversion.

Even the mature Lonergan, however, failed finally to extricate himself from all the fallacies of Marechalian Thomism. To the end, he fallaciously believed that Kantian transcendental logic provides a privileged method for exploring human consciousness. To the end, he defended an inadequate construct of experience that derives ultimately from Kantian epistemology. To the end, he never overcame the intellectualist bias of Thomistic anthropology.

In what follows I shall, then, attempt to argue three interrelated theses: 1) Lonergan's understanding of experience does not have the unchanging normativity he seems to claim for it. 2) Lonergan's notion of experience fails to do justice to intuitive forms of thought and to judgments of feeling that grasp reality in their own right. 3) Despite an inadequate epistemological understanding of experience, what Lonergan calls foundational theological method has the means to correct the inadequacies in Lonergan's epistemology.

Lonergan offers a very restricted definition of the term "experience." By it he means any data that the human mind understands and judges. The mature Lonergan speaks of three different kinds of data corresponding to three different kinds of judgment. Explanatory judgments about events understand the data of sense: namely, sense perceptions and images. Value judgments understand the data provided by feelings about reality, oneself and one's world. Here "data" has echoes of Kant's sense manifold. Transcendental judgments, however, do not deal with sensible realities; instead, they seek to understand the data of consciousness: the operations of the mind before one reflects on them critically.[27]

Moreover, Lonergan's definition of experience rests on a fundamental assumption that grounds his theory of knowledge: namely, the existence of an invariant pattern of operations within human consciousness. Every judgment begins with experience, with the examination of some kind of data. It then proceeds to understanding, which sublates and replaces experience. Finally, judgment about the nature of reality sublates and replaces understanding.[28] In other words, Lonergan discovers the same fundamental cognitive pattern in explanatory, moral, and transcendental judgments. Here two interrelated issues need examination: 1) the method by which Lonergan reaches each of his judgments and 2) the alleged invariance of the pattern of operations that he discovers in all judgments. I turn first to the question of method.

When it comes to interpreting physical phenomena, Lonergan recognizes that scientific method holds the key to insight. Indeed, Lonergan approaches theological method in much the same way that Dewey approaches philosophical method. Both thinkers stand in awe of the accomplishments of contemporary science. Both Dewey the philosopher and Lonergan the theologian realize that the scholarly disciplines that each of them plies differ from scientific thinking with its specialized technology and mathematical precision. Each of them, however, wants to make his discipline approximate better the methods of science.

Dewey, for his part, argues that, if philosophy hopes to advance human insight into life, it must imitate the "denotative" character of scientific thinking. It must begin with the experience of nature, advance to theoretical generalizations about nature, and then return to nature in order to validate or falsify its generalizations.[29] Moreover, Dewey looks to aesthetics, logic, and ethics to provide philosophy with sound norms for thinking.

Lonergan ambitions something similar for theology. Lonergan, for his part, looks to the history of a religious tradition to provide it with the factual data it needs to validate or falsify its hypotheses; and he looks to normative insights into the dynamics of affective, intellectual, moral, and religious conversion to provide theological thinking with its criteria for sound judgment.[30]

Moreover, as I have indicated in an earlier chapter, one finds a convergence between Lonergan's analysis of the fundamental pattern of human thinking, on the one hand, and Peirce's inferential logic on the other. Lonergan argues that a sound rational insight into reality must advance from experience to understanding, from understanding to judgment, and from judgment to decision. Lonergan's notion of "understanding" allows for both a hypothetical and a deductive moment. Peirce, for his part, argues for the irreducibility of hypothetical, deductive, and inductive inference; and he looks to the normative sciences to teach us how to live. Peirce also argues that one cannot validate any hypothesis without interacting with the reality one is trying to understand. At one level, therefore, Lonergan would seem to acknowledge the legitimacy of Peirce's account of scientific method.

In addition, the mature Lonergan holds that judgments of value, moral judgments, differ in content from judgments of fact but that they have fundamentally the same cognitive structure. In ethical thinking one reflects on values, not on facts; but one employs the same operational procedures as one does in scientific thinking.[31]

In exploring the data of consciousness, however, Lonergan gives pride of place, not to scientific paradigms of thought but to Kantian transcendental method. In other words, in his attempt to understand human consciousness, Lonergan substitutes Kantian logic and the Kantian turn to the subject for scientific logic. Each individual must reflect on his or her own consciousness and then decide whether or not the invariant pattern of operations that Lonergan describes occurs there.[32]

In **Insight** Lonergan argues that transcendental method yields a fundamentally unrevisable account of the way the human mind works.[33] The mature Lonergan concedes that one may revise one's account of how the mind works, but that any revision in one's theory of knowledge must conform to the intentional operations of the mind that "underlie" the categories we use to interpret them.[34]

As we have seen, Lonergan holds that human thinking must advance from experience, to understanding, to judgment, and, finally, to decision. He also argues that any attempt to refute this claim must invoke the very pattern of operations he describes in order to mount a refutation. In the process, the refutation refutes itself by assuming the truth of what it is trying to refute.

The mature Lonergan puts it this way:

> A distinction must be drawn between the normative pattern of operations immanent in our consciousness and intentional operations and, on the other hand, objectifications of that pattern in concepts, propositions, words. Obviously, revision can affect nothing but objectifications. It cannot change the dynamic structure of human consciousness.... It follows that there is a sense in which the objectification of the normative pattern of our conscious and intentional operations does not admit revision. The sense in question is that the activity of revising consists in operations in accord with such a pattern, so that a revision rejecting the pattern would be rejecting itself.[35]

Lonergan's argument assumes that human consciousness possesses an invariant dynamic structure, one that "underlies" any normative account of it. One may question the verbalizations and symbolic conceptualizations of this invariant pattern, but one cannot question the pattern itself. No matter how one chooses to talk about the pattern, it itself remains fundamentally unchanged.

Events in nature frequently follow stable patterns no matter how we choose to interpret them. As a consequence, if we take care to think with rational clarity about physical events—if we clarify our hypotheses with deductive precision and then verify or falsify them with care—the events we are investigating will tell us eventually whether or not we have understood them correctly.

Events in physical nature, however, do not occur with self-conscious intentionality. Can we find the same kind of invariance in the conscious acts of the mind? Does the mind work in a uniform way irrespective of the symbolic structures that inform normative thinking about thinking?

I think not. Images, concepts, and symbols enter into the very structure of intentionality itself. They do not supervene on an invariant pattern of mental operations. As the symbolic structures that inform strictly normative human thinking change, the very shape of the mind shifts and evolves.

Peircean logic, for example, prescribes that if one wants to think about reality with rational clarity, one must first formulate an hypothesis, then clarify its operational consequences deductively, and finally validate them inductively by interacting with the reality one is trying to understand. If, with Rahner, one ignores Peirce and opts instead for Kantian logic, then that logic will cause the rational mind to operate in a very different fashion, as a close examination of Rahner's theology proves. Kantian logic teaches the mind to confuse the mere enunciation of an hypothesis with its validation; and this Rahner does with disconcerting frequency every time he discusses the anthropology that subtends his theology.

Despite Lonergan's attempt to restrict the exploration of consciousness to transcendental method, empirical sciences like psychology do investigate the way consciousness evolves. Moreover, empirical investigations of the human mind suggest that it develops in polymorphic rather than in isomorphic ways. The Briggs-Myers test, for example, gives empirical evidence not only that human egos develop different specializations in thinking but that they also manifest an obtuseness when it comes to dealing with those with different cognitive specializations from their own.[36] Thus, those highly specialized in thinking will tend to misunderstand those highly specialized in feeling, and vice versa. Those highly specialized in sensate thinking will tend to misunderstand those highly specialized in intuitive thinking, and vice versa. Introverts and extraverts also process experience differently and can baffle one another.

The polymorphic character of human consciousness makes it impossible to deal adequately with human evaluative responses by using Kantian transcendental method alone. When transcendental Thomists use transcendental method, they tend to assume that the essential sameness of human beings will reveal itself in uniform patterns of cognition. Most transcendental Thomists ground that assumption in faculty psychology. Lonergan continues to defend it even after he has abandoned faculty psychology.

In my judgment, in postulating a pattern of operations that

"underlies" reflective conceptualization, Lonergan confuses ontological with strictly normative invariance. Ontological invariance
characterizes physical events that occur in a uniform way, no matter how one chooses to interpret them hypothetically. Strictly normative invariance, however, prescribes a pattern of intentional
operations as the condition for producing sound cognitive results.
Strictly normative invariance does not, then, describe or even
explain how the mind actually thinks. Rather, it seeks to legislate
the way the mind ought to think.

Lonergan, however, distinguishes between "the normative
pattern immanent in consciousness and intentional operations," on
the one hand, and "objectifications of that pattern of concepts,
propositions, and words," on the other. He also assumes that "revisions can affect nothing but objectifications" of those invariant patterns. Neither the distinction nor the assumption holds water.
Rather, revisions in "objectifications" of consciousness, or normative shifts in one's understanding about the way one ought to think,
change the normative pattern immanent in consciousness and the
intentional operations themselves. In both intuitive and rational
thinking, shifts in method do not leave the mind unchanged. Rather
they deconstruct and reconstruct the mind itself.

An examination of the issues that divine Lonergan's epistemology from that of Ralph Waldo Emerson will, I believe, illustrate
the point I am trying to make. At first glance, the two men would
seem to share little in common philosophically; but closer inspec-
tion reveals more similarity than one would at first presuppose.
Both men made the turn to the subject and used a Kantian logic to
formulate a metaphysical anthropology. Emerson never studied
Kant the way that Lonergan did; but Emerson, like Kant, confused
the formulation of an hypothesis about consciousness with its
demonstration. Moreover, both Emerson and Lonergan claimed to
have reached a normative insight into the way the human mind
grasps reality. Both men claimed to have discovered an invariant
pattern of cognitive operations that yield conscious access to Being.

Unfortunately, however, Emerson's and Lonergan's accounts
of that invariant pattern of cognitive operations contradict one
another. Emerson holds that the human mind grasps reality affec-

tively and intuitively in a way that exceeds any insight available to abstract, rational thinking.[37] Lonergan holds that the human mind grasps Being through a rational abstract inference and that feeling and imaginative intuition only provide the raw materials for both explanatory and moral judgments of reason.[38]

Because Kantian logic confuses the enunciation of an hypothesis with its demonstration, it has no way of resolving the issues dividing Lonergan's from Emerson's epistemology. Both men made the turn to the subject, and both came up with contradictory accounts of the normative pattern of cognitive operations. Lonergan's turn to the subject assures us that, if we inspect the structure of intentionality, we will find that only rational, inferential thinking grasps the real. Emerson assures us that, if we reflect on our own consciousness, we will find that only non-rational intuitive thinking grasps the real.

Lonergan gives abundant evidence of having developed an introverted thinking ego; Emerson gives abundant evidence of having developed an introverted intuitive ego. Both men assumed that everyone who makes the turn to the subject using Kantian logic will find there the same normative pattern of operations. Since, however, they espoused contradictory views of how the human mind ought to think, when they made the turn to the subject each man found there something different. Moreover, both of them ended by making totalitarian claims for his own ego bias.

Worse still, the Kantian logic that grounds the turn to the subject leaves both Lonergan and Emerson bereft of operational procedures to resolve the differences that divide them. When Lonergan tells Emerson that, if he only reflects on his consciousness, he will find there the superiority of rational insight, Emerson can only reply that he finds nothing of the sort. If Emerson challenges Lonergan to find in his consciousness the cognitive superiority of non-rational, intuitive thinking, Lonergan can only reply that he finds there nothing of the sort. In other words, given the polymorphic character of human consciousness, the formulation of an epistemology with no more data than one's own consciousness inevitably transforms any discussion of human cognition into a dialogue of the deaf.

We have, then, good reason to dismiss Lonergan's claim that transcendental method yields a privileged, normative insight into human consciousness. Moreover, the logical inadequacy of transcendental method, its confusion of hypothesis with proof, also undercuts any universal normativity that one might want to attribute to Lonergan's restrictive definition of "experience" as the data one understands and judges. In fact, when Lonergan calls sensations, feelings, and images of reality "data," he merely betrays his Thomistic preference for rational forms of thinking. In the process, he fails to recognize that images and feelings can and do play a far more important role in the human grasp of reality.

Here a comparison of the epistemologies of Peirce, of Lonergan, and of Emerson proves fruitful. Lonergan defines a judgment as "the grasp of the virtually unconditioned."[39] One grasps the virtually unconditioned when one understands the conditions that link one event to another and when one recognizes that those conditions have been fulfilled. In other words, for Lonergan every judgment expresses a rational, inferential interpretation of reality.

As I have already indicated, when it comes to describing abstract, rational thinking, Peirce and Lonergan espouse similar positions, although Peirce, I believe, develops his account of inferential reasoning with greater detail and with more precision than Lonergan. Peirce, however, realized much more clearly than Lonergan did the limitations of abstract, logical thinking. In a sense, Peirce's epistemology validates the contention of G.K. Chesterton that mad people have lost everything but their reason.[40]

Here, I believe, one finds a convergence between Peirce's epistemology and Emerson's. Emerson claimed cognitive pride of place for intuitive judgments of feeling, that they grasp Being in a privileged way that elevates them above abstract, rational inference. Peirce had the good sense to recognize that in dealing with reality one need not choose between rational and intuitive forms of thought. In other words, Peirce's epistemology qualifies and then validates the insights of both Emerson and Lonergan. It validates them by recognizing that the human mind grasps reality with both inferential judgments and with judgments of feeling. It qualifies them by refusing to make totalitarian claims for either form of knowing.

In recognizing the limited role that rational thinking plays in the living of life and in vindicating non-rational ways of grasping the real, Peirce laid remote philosophical foundations for a methodological insight that Bernard Meland, among process theologians, grasps clearly: namely, that we grasp reality both rationally and intuitively, both with inferential, inductive judgments and with judgments of feeling. A balanced theory of knowledge will, therefore, avoid the myopia that characterizes both Emersonian and Lonerganian epistemology by affirming that the human mind has the capacity to grasp reality in both kinds of judgments. Moreover, both kinds of judgments give cognitive access to being.

The mature Lonergan gives greater recognition of the role that feeling plays in human cognition than the Lonergan of **Insight.** Not even the mature Lonergan, however, accords to feeling the capacity to grasp reality as such. Even though he has moved beyond faculty psychology, even the mature Lonergan never overcomes the intellectualist bias of a Thomistic theory of knowledge, which reserves the grasp of reality to the rational intellect alone.

In point of fact, the human mind grasps reality with both inferential judgments and with judgments of feeling. When artists decide that they have finished a work, they do not grasp the virtually unconditioned in the way that Lonergan describes it. The work just feels complete, and the artist knows it.

Feeling also plays an important role in all forms of prudential thinking. Prudential thinking interrelates ideals, decisions, and reality. Human reason may contribute abstract principles to prudential thinking, but those principles provide only general guidelines for action and very rarely tell one how to act in the concrete. One may, for example, espouse a moral principle like: "Never take an innocent human life." But what does innocent mean in the concrete? Does the fact that both the victim of a rape and the child she has conceived qualify as innocent mean that the ravaged woman has to carry the child to term? What if she is retarded? The questions go on and on; and finally the human conscience decides, usually on the basis of a concrete felt sense of the morally fitting response, what course of action will best advance a conflicted moral situation toward the ideals that the conscience affirms as personally binding. The charism of discernment graces such natural processes of prudential reasoning.[41]

I have been arguing that what Lonergan calls transcendental method yields no privileged insight into reality and that his definition of "experience" lacks the normative claims he makes for it. Paradoxically, I reached both of these insights by pursuing what Lonergan calls "foundational theology." Foundational theology in Lonergan's sense of that term calls for a speculatively pluralistic, interdisciplinary investigation of the experience of human conversion. The more I pursued such a theology, the more I realized that such an investigation into the experience of conversion calls into question the epistemological foundations of Lonergan's method. In addition to the difficulties with Lonergan mentioned above, a careful investigation of conversion reveals, for example, that it involves much more than a turn to the subject, as Lonergan seems to suggest.[42] It also involves a turn to the others, as both Dewey's logic and liberation theology insist.[43]

Even though Lonergan himself attempts to ground his theory of method in his epistemology, the fact that his method forces a criticism of his epistemology paradoxically validates it as a method; for any sound method will force the critique of its own presuppositions.

The systematic pursuit of foundational method suggests, then, the need to move beyond Lonergan's restricted definition of "experience" to a more adequate and comprehensive understanding of that term. In the chapter that follows, I shall argue for the importance of using the triadic construct of experience developed by Peirce and Royce in any speculative exploration of human experience in general, of human religious experience, and of the experience of Christian conversion.

Notes

[1]Bernard Lonergan, **Method in Theology** (New York: Herder and Herder, 1972), pp. 130-31, 237-47, 267-93.

[2]Karl Rahner, **Foundations of Christian Faith: An Introduction to**

the Idea of Christianity, translated by William F. Dych (New York: Seabury, 1978), pp. 44-89.

[3]Karl Rahner, Spirit in the World, translated by William F. Dych, S.J. (Montreal: Palm Publishers, 1968); Hearers of the Word, translated by Michael Richards (New York: Herder and Herder, 1969); Foundations, pp. 1-89.

[4]Bernard Lonergan, Insight: A Study of Human Understanding (New York: Philosophical Library, 1956), pp. 33-139.

[5]Karl Rahner, Spirit in the World, pp. 188ff.

[6]Karl Rahner, S.J., Schriften zur Theologie (Cologne: Benziger, 1961ff), V, pp. 183ff.

[7]DS 3135-40.

[8]Lonergan, Method, pp. 340-44.

[9]Jean Piaget, Insights and Illusions of Philosophy, translated by Wolf Mays (New York: Meridian, 1971).

[10]Cf. Donald L. Gelpi, S.J., Grace as Transmuted Experience and Social Process: And Other Essays in North American Philosophy (Lanham: University Press of America, 1988), pp. 67-95.

[11]Karl Rahner, Foundations, pp. 51-55.

[12]In Thomistic Aristotelianism, all productive activity flows from the powers of the substance, not from the substance directly. That leaves Thomism without an adequate explanation for the origin of the powers of the soul. Aquinas recognized the difficulty and argued that the powers of the soul simply "flow from the essence of the soul as a source (fluunt ab essentia sicut ab principio)," and that this "emanation (emanatio)" happens "through a kind of natural resultancy (per aliquam naturalem resultantiam)." (Summa Theologiae, I, q. lxxvii, q. 6). One suspects from the strained character of the angelic doctor's answer that he himself had given only a verbal and not a real solution to a perplexing philosophical problem.

[13]Rahner, Spirit in the World, pp. 132-236.

[14]Summa Theologiae, I, q. lxxviii, a. 3, q. lxxxi, a. 2.

[15]Rahner, Spirit in the World, pp. 120-45.

[16]I do not fault Thomism for distinguishing different kinds of knowing. I find fault with distinguishing the powers of the soul by formal objects that so separate the powers of the soul from one another that they have to move one another to act. Human experience when closely examined has more continuity than that. It makes much more sense to me to speak of a continuum of feeling stretching from concrete sensory experiences (which already have emotional coloring) into feeling and affectively col-

ored images that clarify feeling intuitively and finally into the different forms of inference. Inferential thinking overlaps with intuitive, since hypothetical inference invokes intuitive patterns of thinking. The continuity of human evaluation makes it seem unlikely to me that human evaluative responses result from essentially distinct powers of the soul pushing one another around. Rather they seem to result from interrelated and sometimes overlapping habitual tendencies. Cf. Donald L. Gelpi, **Experiencing God: A Theology of Human Emergence** (Lanham: University Press of America, 1987), pp. 75-97. See also Charles Hartshorne, **The Philosophy and Psychology of Sensation** (Chicago: University of Chicago Press, 1945).

[17]Rahner, **Foundations,** pp. 55-57; **Theological Investigations** (Baltimore: Helicon, 1954), I, pp. 297-346.

[18]Donald L. Gelpi, S.J., **Life and Light: A Guide to the Theology of Karl Rahner** (New York: Sheed and Ward, 1966).

[19]Rahner never says as such that every infant in the womb has a supernatural existential; but its presence in an unborn child would seem to flow from the fact that God builds the supernatural into the **a priori** structure of the human spirit.

[20]Rahner, **Schriften zur Theologie,** V, pp. 156-58.

[21]For a discussion of the philosophical presuppositions that underlie these reflections, see Gelpi, **Experiencing God,** pp. 52-121.

[22]Cf. John H. Flavell, **The Developmental Psychology of Jean Piaget** (New York: Van Nostrand, 1963); Donald L. Gelpi, S.J., **Grace as Transmuted Experience and Social Process,** pp. 1-40.

[23]For further discussion of this point, see Gelpi, **Experiencing God,** pp. 122-52.

[24]Cf. Gelpi, **Grace as Transmuted Experience and Social Process,** pp. 67-95.

[25]Bernard J.F. Lonergan, **Insight: A Study of Human Understanding** (New York: Philosophical Library, 1956), pp. 634-86; **Method in Theology,** pp. 267-94, 343.

[26]Lonergan, **Method,** pp. 237-44.

[27]Lonergan, **Insight,** pp. 72-74, 235-36, 274, 333-35; **Method,** pp. 38, 64-66, 72, 86, 94, 201-02.

[28]Lonergan, **Insight,** pp. 271-316; **Method,** pp. 6-13.

[29]John Dewey, **Experience and Nature** (La Salle: Open Court, 1971), pp. 8, 33-34, 60.

[30]Lonergan, **Method,** pp. 125-45.

[31]Lonergan, **Method,** pp. 36-40.

[32]**Ibid.,** pp. 13-25.

[33]Lonergan, **Insight,** pp. 335-36.

[34]Lonergan, **Method,** pp. 10-20.

[35]**Ibid.**

[36]For an introduction to the Briggs-Myers test, see Alan W. Brownsword, **It Takes All Types!** (Fairfax: Van Norman/Associates, 1987).

[37]See Donald L. Gelpi, S.J., **Endless Seeker: The Religious Quest of Ralph Waldo Emerson** (Lanham: University Press of America, 1991).

[38]Lonergan, **Method,** pp. 4-40.

[39]Lonergan, **Insight,** pp. 280-81.

[40]Charles Sanders Peirce, **Collected Papers,** edited by Charles Hartshorne and Paul Weiss (8 vols.; Cambridge: Harvard, 1931ff), 1.616-77.

[41]For a more detailed and technical argument of this point, see Donald L. Gelpi, S.J., **Inculturating North American Theology: An Experiment in Scientific Method** (Atlanta: Scholars Press, 1988), pp. 49-97.

[42]Lonergan defines "conversion" as a decision that creates a horizon. Cf. Lonergan, **Method,** pp. 237-44. The definition tells only a half truth since it confines its concern to the intentional structure of human subjectivity. Lonergan's definition of conversion reflects, in other words, his transcendental turn to the subject. As a consequence, it fails to capture a fundamental fact about conversion, that it involves a turning from and a turning to. A social conception of conversion as the shift from irresponsible to responsible behavior in some realm of experience seems to me to capture better the experience of conversion. Cf. Gelpi, **Grace as Transmuted Experience and Social Process,** pp. 97-139.

[43]Gelpi, **Inculturating North American Theology,** pp. 99-146.

5

The Importance and Promise of a Triadic Construct of Experience

In the preceding chapters I have examined some of the principal, contemporary attempts to make the theological turn to experience. I have argued that those attempts have produced mixed and often enough negative theological results. Before examining the importance and promise of a triadic construct of experience, we should, perhaps, review the preceding analysis and take stock of our progress.

As we have seen, Schillebeeckx correctly situates the interpretation of an experience within the experience itself. He also correctly recognizes the social and linguistic conditioning of all such interpretations. Unfortunately, however, he also espouses a di-polar construct of experience that betrays him into conceptual nominalism. Given, however, Schillebeeckx's sensitivity to the social dimensions of experience and given his desire to avoid Kantian solipsism, one may legitimately regard him as a conceptual nominalist aspiring toward realism.

Having decided, however, to understand experience in vaguely Kantian terms as the subjective interrelation of concrete percepts and abstract concepts, Schillebeeckx finds himself hard pressed to discourse about any religious experience other than apophatic mysticism and a subjective experience of grace. The rationalistic cast of his understanding of interpretation also prevents him from dealing adequately with the intuitive patterns of narrative and poetic thinking in the New Testament.

Moreover, Schillebeeckx's conceptual nominalism keeps him from interpreting adequately the resurrection appearances, which the New Testament describes as encounters with the risen Christ.

Instead, Schillebeeckx presents resurrection faith as an inference based on a Spirit-inspired, subjective sense of personal salvation.

Moreover, the conceptual nominalism that lies at the basis of Schillebeeckx's attempt to lay New Testament foundations for Christology betrays him into avoiding any extensive discussion of New Testament Christology as such. His first volume deals with primarily Jesusology, with the mortal ministry of Jesus. Moreover, as just noted, it also fails to deal adequately with the resurrection encounters that ground New Testament Christological faith. Schillebeeckx's second volume deals with a New Testament theology of grace, and touches on Christology only in passing. The third volume summarizes the first two and appends wise reflections on democratizing the church. In other words, despite the awesome scholarship that Schillebeeckx displays, one may legitimately argue that, in the course of his three volumes, he manages rather astonishingly to avoid discussion of New Testament Christology.

In examining the role that praxis and the turn to experience play in Latin American liberation theology, we discerned the presence of both Kantian and Thomistic presuppositions. Transcendental Thomism has colored and obscured the attempt of liberation theologians to deal with the relationship between orthodoxy and orthopraxis. Clodovis Boff has produced the most extensive treatment of that relationship. As we saw, however, he falls into the same conceptual nominalism as Schillebeeckx. Moreover, his portrayal of theology as a purely speculative discipline prevents him from offering a satisfying account of how orthodoxy and orthopraxis relate to one another.

Process theology manages to avoid the fallacies of Kantian transcendental logic, but it too embraces a conceptual nominalism, despite the Platonic caste of Whitehead's cosmology. Moreover, Whitehead's conceptual nominalism combines with his atomistic account of the growth of experience in ways that lead to several philosophical dead ends.

Whitehead's atomistic, nominalistic universe lacks a motor. It cannot explain adequately the most basic category in Whitehead's categoreal scheme: namely, "creativity." Despite his insistence on the primacy of relationship, Whitehead fails finally to explain human interpersonal relationships, offers an inadequate philosophy of person, and lacks the categories to explain adequately interpersonal and institutional relationships. Whitehead's ontologism fails to do justice to the variety and complexity of human religious experience.

In examining the attempts of Protestant process theologians to deal with Christian doctrine, we found them repeatedly acquiescing in Whitehead's rationalistic presuppositions and, as a consequence, espousing an attenuated form of Arianism and unitarianism. They also repeatedly confound the order of creation and the order of grace and redemption. Moreover, since Whitehead's atomistic nominalism keeps each actual occasion of any experience from ever experiencing the future as such, the philosophy of organism has subverted the attempts of Protestant process theologians to deal adequately with Christian eschatology. Joseph Bracken's attempt to think Catholic orthodoxy within a Whiteheadean frame of reference, while genuine in its search for orthodox formulas, at times falls short of its laudable purpose. Moreover, Bracken's attempt to combine Royce and Whitehead fails to take into account their contradictory constructs of experience. As a consequence, Bracken's attempt to import Royce's philosophy of interpretation into Whitehead's nominalistic universe lacks logical consistency and coherence.

Finally, in reflecting on the turn to experience in transcendental Thomism, I argued that Kantian transcendental logic combines with the presuppositions of classical metaphysics in order to betray Rahner into an inadequate, prescriptive approach to human religious experience.

I have also argued that two philosophical failures lie at the basis of the preceding theological confusions: 1) the failure to take into account C.S. Peirce's critique of the inadequacies of Kantian logic, Peirce's theory of inference, his triadic phenomenology of experience, his epistemology, and his nascent, realistic metaphysics; 2) the failure to acknowledge Josiah Royce's attempts to build on Peirce's philosophical foundations in order to develop a metaphysics of community coordinate with the faith experience of Christians.

The time has come to try to build on the insights of Peirce and of Royce that I have alluded to in the preceding argument. If these gentlemen have the right of it (and in my judgment they do), then only a realistic, triadic, communitarian construct of human experience can do justice to Christian revelation.

Moreover, in reflecting on the achievement of these two giants of the American philosophical tradition, I have argued for a convergence between their thought and selected aspects of the mature Lonergan's reflections on theological method. I have argued that despite Lonergan's failure to extricate himself fully from the presuppositions and fallacies of Kantian logic and epistemology, nevertheless his theory of method points the way to advancing methodologically beyond the inadequacies of transcendental logic. In describing the task of foundational theology, Lonergan calls for a multi-disciplinary investigation of human religious experience that takes into account the insights of philosophy, of theology, and of any other relevant sciences that examine the nature of human experience in general and of human religious experience in particular. Here I find a convergence between Lonergan's method and the method of Jean Piaget.

In the present chapter, I would like to test the ability of a realistic, triadic, communitarian construct of experience to advance the work of foundational theology. My argument divides into three parts. The first argues for the philosophical adequacy of Peirce's triadic model of experience. In this first section of my argument, I shall try to show that a triadic construct of experience promises to interpret and integrate into itself the best insights of other philosophical constructs of experience.

In the second part of my argument, I shall argue that a realistic, triadic, communitarian construct of experience, analogous to that proposed to by Royce, promises to interpret the results of those other sciences besides philosophy and theology that examine human experience and human religious institutions and behavior.

In the third part of my argument, I shall attempt to show that a realistic, triadic, communitarian construct of experience promises to interpret the three central mysteries of the Christian faith: the

Trinity, the incarnation, and the Breath-inspired church of Jesus Christ.

I have called this chapter "The Importance and Promise of a Triadic Construct of Experience." Like Whitehead's philosophy of organism, I shall propose an understanding of experience that aspires to metaphysical universality. Nevertheless, because a Peircean logic of inference validates that construct, unlike Rahner's transcendental Thomism, the metaphysics of experience I shall propose claims no **a priori,** necessary grasp of being. True to its Peircean roots, my triadic construct of experience professes a contrite fallibilism. It eschews any claims to necessity, even though it aspires to universality. As a consequence, others may well come up with better, more comprehensive constructs. I offer this one, however, because, after testing it out in a variety of ways, I believe it holds genuine speculative promise.

Allow me to underline the term "promise." As Whitehead saw clearly, any world hypothesis, including the one I shall propose, can aspire to applicability and adequacy but cannot guarantee it. If, however, the hypothesis hopes to gain other adherents, it must at least promise the possibility of universal applicability. That promise, if initially justified, gives the hypothesis its speculative importance; for, if it should in fact prove to have the universality to which it aspires, it will have the capacity to endow theoretical religious insight with the unifying, synthetic character to which it aspires.

I am afraid that, in a confused age of theological eclecticism, many theologians and students of theology have despaired of systematic thinking and settle for a grab-bag of dubiously related theological ideas. The integrating character of religious insight demands, however, that all speculative theology aspire to a synthetic insight and therefore to a systematic one.

All religious thinking seeks a synthetic, and therefore a systematic, insight into reality because it seeks an explanation of the real that puts one in a life-giving, saving relationship with oneself, with other persons, with God, and with the world. Such an insight needs to think truly about world, self, other persons, and God: in other words, about anything at all. The metaphysical mind generates such insights. Any genuine religious experience will, then, at some point need a metaphysics to give it abstract, synthetic unity. Whitehead correctly identified the normative traits of such a metaphysics. Only a logical, coherent, applicable, and adequate construct of experience will yield the kind of insight that gives a theological account of reality the kind of abstract, theoretical unity it needs.

Let us then begin to test the promise of a realistic, triadic, communitarian construct of experience to function as synthetic religious metaphysics. In what follows, I shall draw on insights of Peirce, Royce, and other major thinkers in the North American philosophical tradition. I offer the following construct of experience, however, not as an exegesis of their thought but as an expression of my own mind.

(I)

What, then, do I mean by a triadic, realistic, communitarian construct of experience?

A triadic construct of experience defines experience as a process made up of relational elements called feelings. It discovers three generic variables in the higher forms of experience: evaluations, actions, and tendencies. It may in fact prove true that some kind of primitive evaluation functions in the most elemental physical reactions, as Whitehead's philosophy of organism suggests; but a triadic construct of experience leaves that question open and looks to the physical sciences to provide the hard evidence that would validate or invalidate such an hypothesis. Perhaps Whitehead has hypothesized correctly. On the other hand, very primitive, physical reactions could conceivably engage only two variables, not three: laws (or tendencies) and actions. Such a process would, however, still fit the preceding definition of experience. Let us, however, focus on the higher forms of experience that contain three, not two, identifiable forms of feelings.[1]

In human consciousness, the realm of value develops in a continuum of conceptual feelings. Intentional relations unite evaluative responses since every evaluation expresses the feeling of something possible, actual, or real. In and of themselves, evaluations express only possibility, but they also express the way we become present to actual activity and to real tendency in ourselves and in others. For example, the concept blue exemplifies a pure possibility of color; but viewing the painting "The Blue Boy" yields different sensations of blue which make the picture present to us and us to it.

Sensations of touch, of sight, of smell, of sound, and of taste combine with proprio-sensations of bodily comfort, discomfort, motion, and position to create the first complex realm of human evaluative response. Because in sensing we respond to the actual physical impact of things upon us, sensations yield a strong sense of factual givenness. Nevertheless, close studies of human sensation reveal them as emotionally tinged. Moreover, if we allow our emotional responses to ourselves and our impinging world to develop, they begin to disclose to us the tendencies present in things. The fact that sensations already have emotional meaning shows, then, that they yield an extremely vague but nevertheless real cognitive grasp of tendency.

As our emotional responses to things develop, we perceive in a preliminary way the tendencies present in them. I respond to a coiled snake with fear because I perceive its potential to harm me; I rejoice at seeing a friend because I anticipate a deepening of the bond that unites us.

Images—whether remembered, reconstructed, imagined, or archetypal—illumine emotional responses and can clarify or confuse our affective grasp of tendency. The sight of the coiled snake may remind one of others who have suffered or even died of snakebite; and their imagined or remembered ordeal may reinforce one's apprehension. Similarly, memories of past joys may enhance the pleasure of a chance encounter with a friend.

Intuitive thinking engages the interplay of feelings and images in order to grasp reality. Moreover, the human attempt to interpret and communicate intuitive feelings helps give them intentional structure. Lyrics, narratives of all kinds, music, the visual and kinetic arts, drama—all such artistic interpretations of intuitive insights into the real educate and give shape to the intuitive mind.

The interplay of image and feeling eventually gives rise to a felt judgment about the kinds of tendencies present in realities about which one thinks intuitively. For example, the sight of a coiled rattler on the jogging path could remind me of my friend who lost three fingers from the bite of a baby rattler with which he was foolishly playing. On the basis of that memory I might on the sight of the snake turn immediately and flee. If I postpone decision, however, I might recall other wilderness encounters with snakes: I may remind myself of how they seem as inclined to avoid humans as humans them, or I may recall the hike in the Grand Canyon of the Toulumne when we had to skirt three rattlers on the trail without problem or injury. On the basis of these and similar recollections, I may reach the prudential judgment that fleeing the coiled snake amounts to an overreaction and that I should continue my jog, but keep a safe distance from the serpent's jaws.

We reach such prudential judgments hundreds of times in the course of a day. The perplexed conscience uses them to resolve situations of conflicting moral claims. Artists use judgments of feeling to assess whether their artistic performance communicates the intuitive insight that grips them personally.

Intuitive thinking does not follow logical rules, for it has other methods: memory, free imaginative association, synchronicity, connotation, metaphor, to name a few. The skillful use of such methods can, moreover, grasp and name events with accuracy, lucidity, and emotional power.

The higher forms of sensate animal life give evidence of memory and intuitive insight. Dogs can learn manners in an obedience school, porpoises and seals can learn to turn spontaneous play into acrobatics. As animal life shades down into less complex forms, however, evaluative response probably shades down into unconscious response. Do, for example, oysters have emotional lives? If they did, how would we know?

In the higher forms of intuitive thinking that humans engage in, one can, moreover, discern a variety of images that give it intentional structure: spontaneous memories that resemble sensory after-images in their quasi-givenness, reconstructed memories of things one finds hard to recall, imitative images like follow the leader, creative fantasy, and archetypal images. The latter have special interest because, by their elemental human associations and emotional power, they organize the human imagination in discernible patterns that surface in different individuals, eras, and cultures.

Rational and intuitive thinking overlap, for hypothetical thinking, which begins the process of rational investigation, results from mind play, from free association and from playful fantasy, rather than from rational thought. Speculative models provide the hypothetical mind with metaphors for reality that generate creative hypotheses. Hypothetical thinking, however, drives in a different direction from artistic intuition; for hypothesis seeks not the expression of an intuition as such but a rationally defined classification of unexplained data that will allow one to predict how it will behave. For example, after atomic scientists had decided to imagine the atom as a small solar system, they could begin to predict with some precision how its particles might or might not act in measurable ways.

Hypothetical thinking, as we saw in Chapter 2, classifies rationally unexplained factual data on the basis of a rule that it assumes to govern their operation. Deductive thinking clarifies the implications of a hypothesis by predicting, on the basis of the assumed rule, that the realities under investigation will act in specific ways under specifiable circumstances. Inductive thinking verifies an hypothesis when, on the basis of the appearance of the predicted data, it concludes, when successful, that the rule that the original hypothesis assumed as the basis of its inference, actually interprets the real laws or tendencies present in things.

Besides controlled experimental thinking, the human mind also engages in scholarship, which normally blends inference and intuition. Historical thinking illustrates how the scholarly mind works. The historian must, on the basis of personal accounts of past events and of historical artifacts, reconstruct a chronicle of the events it must then explain. The historian explains the order of those historical events by identifying the decisive ones that caused history to take this rather than that. Literary and artistic criticism clearly blends intuitive and rational insights into reality; for one needs intuitive insight to understand the works of art or literature one is studying as well as the rational skills of an historian in order to contextualize those works.

Finally, the human mind also engages in strictly normative thinking when it measures its own behavior against ideals, principles, and realities that one has interiorized as personally binding. One can, for example, reflect self-critically on the adequacy of one's methods for dealing practically with other persons or things or with social institutions; or one can reflect on the health of one's personal emotional development, on the way one ought to think about reality, whether intuitively or rationally, on questions of conscience, and on questions of religious belief, attitude, and commitment.

Like intuitive thinking, all forms of rational thinking exhibit linguistic, cultural, and social conditioning. I suspect that only the mathematical mind thinks with pure reason as it predicts and validates the operational consequences of different abstract symbol systems. Any thinking that uses ordinary language, however rationally refined, may aspire to pure rationality but will probably fall short of it. Ordinary language has too many sensate, affective, and imaginative associations and connotations to communicate in a purely rational way.

If one reflects on the whole gamut of human evaluative responses four general characteristics stand out: 1) Human evaluative responses develop in a conceptual continuum that stretches from sensation to the higher forms of abstract thinking. 2) Human evaluative responses make us present to ourselves and to our world. 3) Human evaluative responses supply the temporal dimension to spatio-temporal experience. 4) The three kinds of feeling—evaluations, actions, and tendencies—all mutually condition one another and contribute to the process of ongoing self-definition. Let us reflect on each of these points in turn.

1) The presence of a conceptual continuum in human evaluative response makes faculty psychology inherently improbable, in my judgment. Instead of resulting from essentially distinct powers of the soul moving one another to act, human evaluations seem to result from blending and overlapping of different habitual tenden-

cies. Abstract ideas, for example, have emotional and imaginative connotations because intuitive habits link rational thinking more or less consciously to human intuitive responses.

2) We become present to the world by responding to it evaluatively. If the freezing water I am wading in desensitizes my foot to pain, I may not become present to the fact that I have cut it until warmth restores sensitivity and the wound begins to ache. When my foot aches, then, my unconscious wound enters my consciousness as localized pain.

3) Similarly, memory makes past events present in consciousness. The affective and imaginative perception of tendencies yields an intuitive sense of how they will probably act and begins to turn my present perception of them into an anticipated future. Rational thinking endows such temporal perception with logical precision. When I formulate a rational hypothesis about a reality I become present to it in a new way because I have defined it in a way that allows me to predict its behavior with greater conceptual precision. In deductive thinking the hypothetical present begins to turn into a future as I anticipate the way that the thing I am investigating will act. In inductive thinking, the predicted future becomes a present as I validate or invalidate my hypotheses on the basis of the appearance or non-appearance of anticipated behavior.

Scholarly thinking also endows experience with greater rational and intuitive precision. History, for example, gives communities of memory a causal account of how they have evolved and makes them more systematically present to their past. Self-critical thinking, by contrast, gives one present access to the kind of future to which one ought to aspire.

If evaluative response gives experience its temporal character, the realities to which we respond create the environment in which we respond and give experience its spatial character. We experience other persons and things when they act upon us physically and decisively. The terms "physically" and "decisively" here mean the same thing.

4) Physical action makes experience concrete: it determines a developing experience to be this rather than that. When action terminates an evaluation, it expresses the kind of evaluation it termi-

nates. I may act lovingly or hatefully, rationally or intuitively, responsibly or unthinkingly.

Moreover, every action either creates a new tendency to act or reinforces an old one. Every time I fix my beliefs about reality, whether rationally or intuitively, I build into myself a tendency to respond to persons or things in predictable ways. The burned child tends to fear fire and with good reason. Similarly, once I decide that I have made a friend, I will cease to treat the person in question with suspicion or hostility. If I tend to blow up, every time I throw a tantrum, I reinforce my tendency to explode. By the same token, every time I perform a genuine act of kindness I build the virtue of kindness into my character. Finally, every action tends to generate a specific kind of evaluative or decisive response.

Acting selves inhabit the environments we experience. By a "self" I mean merely "an autonomously functioning tendency to act or to respond in some way." Tendencies function autonomously when they initiate their own activity; they cease to function autonomously when a larger reality that has absorbed them rules their decisions efficaciously. Think, for example, of the organic chemicals that make up the human body. Once absorbed through the digestive process, they function, not as autonomous selves but as integral parts of a complex human self. They follow laws but they do not act as autonomous selves.

Every autonomous self creates itself through interaction with its world. Action does not merely modify the self accidentally. It creates the very self anew by building into it novel, habitual functioning tendencies or by reinforcing old ones. In a world of triadic experiences, habits, then, subsist when they function autonomously. Moreover, the self-creative dimension of a triadic experience means that selves emerge from their bodies, they do not subsist in them like some fixed, unchanging substantial essence.

The body provides the most immediate environment from which the self emerges. It consists of physically assimilated parts of the larger environment with which the self interacts. Physical assimilation successfully incorporates elements of one's world into one's total self in ways that sustain existence. Food recreates the body. Digestion sustains growth and perpetuates vital functions.

The body, then, anchors one in a world, in an enveloping environment of interacting physical forces of different degrees of consciousness and complexity. Anyone who has experienced the wilderness knows that the gross forces of nature—storms, rushing streams, earthquakes—act not with malice but with unconscious indifference to the survival of life. Plants produce both nourishing and toxic fruit. Animals on whom we prey fear us; animals that prey on us terrify us. Communities of persons, however, constitute the most significant and sustaining forces in the human environment.

As selves, persons function autonomously. As living selves, they develop in vital continuity with the selves they have already become in the course of their lives. Persons differ from other living selves in their capacity to convert, i.e. to assume self-conscious responsibility for their own personal growth and development in some realm of experience. Conversion presupposes, then, the relational character of persons; for responsibility means social accountability to other persons; and social accountability demands the capacity to respond to other persons as persons.

Human communities nurture consciousness in the new persons born or accepted into them. As a consequence, all human activity exhibits social conditioning. Responsible communities seek to nurture new members to the moment of conversion in community, i.e. to the moment of adult maturity when the member of the community can assume full responsibility for the community as such and for his or her development within it. Since every human culture blends and institutionalizes both insight and illusion, both virtue and malice, both truth and lies, both life-giving and oppressive institutions, adult conversion cannot happen until younger members of a community not only assimilate but then move beyond the community's conventional wisdom to critical reflection upon it.

Religious communities know that the total environment in which human experiences grow and develop includes God, because as the supremely perfect, all-encompassing reality, God subsists as that reality in which we live, move, and have our being. When created, spatio-temporal realities touch us, we interact with them; when God touches us, we encounter the holy. The certitude of faith results from an awareness of the fact of God's touch. The development of faith results from the attempt to interpret the significance and consequences of that touch.

The forms of conversion correspond to distinct but interrelated realms of human experience. Realms of experience differ by the kind of habits or tendencies that function within them. In every developing experience, moreover, one must distinguish the autonomous selves that inhabit one's experienced world from the self that does the experiencing. One can, then, take responsibility for the development of one's world, and one can take responsibility for the development of oneself. That means that one can respond with five different generic kinds of habits, each capable of self-reflective direction and control: habits of personal emotional response, habits of intuitive and rational interpretation, habits of personal moral conduct, habits of public moral conduct, habits of faith.

We can therefore speak of five kinds of conversion: 1) Affective conversion promotes healthy personal emotional development. 2) Intellectual conversion promotes true beliefs about reality, whether one reaches those beliefs intuitively or rationally. 3) Personal moral conversion ensures responsible interpersonal relationships. 4) Socio-political conversion promotes the ongoing reform of unjust social structures. 5) Religious conversion responds to the divine touch on the terms set by God.

Although the adult human person responds with self-critical responsibility in five different but interrelated realms of experience, personal conversion differs notably from socio-political. The four forms of personal conversion—affective, theoretical, moral, and religious—all concern themselves directly with the converting self and with the kind of self it ought to choose to become. In socio-political conversion, one takes responsibility for the natural and social environment in which one lives and for the responsible development of the institutions that shape that environment.

One must speak of the conversion not only of persons but of communities as such. Fully converted communities institutionalize patterns of behavior that foster all five forms of conversion in its members. Unconverted communities institutionalize neurosis or psychosis, lies and propaganda, moral selfishness, religious unbelief, and institutional irresponsibility. Converted communities enlighten and liberate their members. Unconverted communities confuse and oppress their members. As a consequence, in both communities and individual persons both consciousness and freedom flicker.

Personal consciousness differs from the shared consciousness of communities. Finite personal consciousness emerges with the capacity to distinguish between one's own body and the surrounding environment. Personal consciousness grows the more one can distinguish realities from one another and grasp the way that distinguished realities interrelate. Community consciousness grows through a much more complex process of corporate historical reappropriation and self-direction. Communities become initially conscious of themselves as communities by reaching a consensus about the significance of the events that found them and of the history that links them to those events. Consensus about its historical origins endows a community with a shared sense of identity; but shared consciousness grows as a community further decides on the basis of its historical sense of identity the kind of community it ought to become and then mobilizes the gifts of all its members to transform that future into a reality.

The focused character of finite consciousness corresponds to the needs and interests of the developing self. As needs and interests shift, the searchlight of consciousness swings from one reality to another. Peripheral consciousness surrounds focal consciousness. Focal consciousness centers on matters of immediate importance; peripheral consciousness contains realities and values that we acknowledge but prefer not to deal with for the moment. Moreover, peripheral consciousness shades off into the pre-conscious: i.e. into unconscious experiences, memories and attitudes capable of recall. Beyond the pre-conscious lies the unconscious: experiences, memories, and attitudes that resist conscious recall. Conscious exploration of the pre-conscious and of the unconscious enhances personal self-understanding.

Freedom consists in the ability to discriminate realistic possibilities of acting and in the ability to effect one rather than the other. Freedom flickers with environment, with the capacity to distinguish realistic options for choice, with the capacity to view reality from a variety of frames of reference, with cultivated skills that empower different kinds of activity, and with cultivated tastes and desires that condition one's preferences. The degree of conversion present in individuals and communities will also condition the freedom with which both can act with self-conscious responsibility. Moreover, the different forms of personal and of communal conversion all mutually condition one another.

The preceding categoreal scheme sketches the realistic, triadic, communal construct of experience that I am proposing in this chapter for philosophical, scientific, and theological testing. The scheme conceives experience realistically by recognizing the reality of general tendencies to act or respond in identifiable ways. It conceives experience as triadic by identifying three generic, mutually interrelated variables in the development of the higher forms of experience: particular evaluations, concrete actions, and general tendencies. It conceives experience socially by recognizing that the persons, things, and communities we experience stand within experience, not outside it, and help make it into the kind of experience it eventually becomes.

In the sections of this chapter that follow I shall attempt to test in a preliminary way the philosophical, scientific, and theological promise of this construct.

(II)

The preceding categoreal scheme aspires to logical consistency, coherence, applicability, and adequacy. I myself find no logical inconsistencies in the preceding scheme, but I profess myself open to correction on that score.

As for coherence, the key terms—"experience," "process," "feelings," "relationship," "evaluations," "actions," and "tendencies"—all mutually imply one another. As a descriptive expansion of these interrelated categories the rest of the scheme seems to me to cohere as well.

Moreover, the coherence of the triadic construct of experience also appears in this: that it manages to avoid the dualisms that have traditionally plagued western philosophy. Dualistic conceptions of reality distinguish and describe interrelated realities in ways that make their very real relationship to one another subsequently unintelligible.

A triadic construct of experience avoids spirit-matter dualism by replacing the metaphysical terms "spirit" and "matter" with experiential language of relationship. Dualistic conceptions of spirit and of matter do not surface in a triadic construct of experience, because it offers a descriptive account of experience that never uses these confused and troublesome categories. Moreover, the construct insists on the fundamental interrelatedness of all the variables that give experience its dynamic structure. At the same time, it allows both for negative relations of distinction and for negative destructive relationships.

A triadic construct of experience avoids operational dualism by refusing to define some faculties as essentially spiritual and others as merely organic. Instead a triadic construct of experience discovers a continuum of evaluative response stretching from basic sensory experience to abstract modes of thinking; and it portrays the growth of consciousness as the acquisition of increasingly complex patterns of perception and of interpretation. It also discovers a conceptual continuum linking the conscious and unconscious mind. Moreover, it grounds evaluative response in a developing, unified pattern of habits.

A triadic construct of experience avoids subjectivism by insisting that the realities we know stand within experience, not outside it, and help in this way to define the character of any given experience. In other words, things exist in one another to the extent that they experience one another.

A triadic construct of experience avoids individualism in three ways. First, it conceives each human self as relational and social in its intrinsic constitution. Second, it asserts that individuals achieve personal identity in part by appropriating the traditions of the communities to which they belong. Third, a triadic construct of experience insists that individuals come to full adulthood by critical reflection on any inadequacies in their community's received wisdom and by commitment to collaborating with others to correct those inadequacies.

Finally, as we shall see in more detail below, experience viewed as traidic avoids time-eternity dualism by portraying God as the supreme exemplification of experience, as an eternal process within which the spatio-temporal process develops.

If, then, a triadic construct of experience gives promise of logical consistency and coherence, what of its applicability and adequacy? One may test the interpretative adequacy of a philosophical construct of experience in a variety of ways. Most obviously, one may compare it with other philosophical constructs of experience to see whether it can take into account the kinds of issues they raise and whether it corrects any inadequacies into which they might have fallen.

In the preface to this book, I called "experience" a weasel word and distinguished at least six possible meanings of the term. After qualifying each of these terms, a triadic construct of experience finds a truth in all of them.

A triadic construct of experience recognizes in the practical wisdom that comes from more or less prolonged exposure to some reality one example of experience, but not an exhaustive account of it. The same holds true for the two restricted definitions of "experience" that Lonergan offers. Sensory realities and the operations of the mind prior to critical reflection upon them only exemplify particular experiences, but they fail to provide an adequate or exhaustive definition of experience.

If with Dewey one extends the term to include the whole spectrum of human evaluative responses, once again one identifies one important realm of experience—namely, evaluation—but one fails to provide an exhaustive description of experience. Why? Because experience has both a what and a how. We experience reality in a certain way by the kind of evaluative response we bring to it; but the realities we experience stand within experience, not outside it.

A triadic construct of experience agrees therefore with Whitehead that any adequate philosophical account of experience will transform it into a term universally applicable in intent; but it replaces Whitehead's di-polar, atomic, nominalistic construct of experience with a triadic, communitarian, realistic one. Nevertheless, a construct of experience defines "being" or "reality" as experience, which in turn divides into what we experience and the way that we experience it. What we experience divides into concrete actions that forge social links among experiences and into the autonomously functioning selves that act and evaluate.

Finally, a triadic construct of experience acknowledges both conscious and unconscious evaluations and therefore asserts the existence of an unconscious mind. However, a triadic construct of experience leaves it to positive science to decide the question whether the more primitive forms of experience—purely physical processes and plants—give behavioral evidence of unconscious evaluations or not.

In a lucid and clarifying article in **Theological Studies**, George Schner distinguishes four major philosophical models of experience: experience as construct, experience as intentional, experience as derivative, and experience as dialectical.[2] How do these models compare with a triadic construct of experience?

By experience as construct Schner means "interior and exterior awareness" explored through the mediation of "memory or imagination, through thought by means of conceptualization or judgment, through language by means of articulation, or through symbolic representation of some kind." Any appeal to "experience" in this philosophical understanding of the term acknowledges the revisability of that appeal, since experience exemplifies a construction of the mind.

In experience understood as construct, one can, therefore, never speak of experience as given, as unmediated, as incorrigible, or atomistic. The fallibility of constructions makes them corrigible. Their construction by the mind precludes their givenness and entails their mediated character. The flow of consciousness rules out an atomistic interpretation of experience.[3]

When compared with a triadic construct of experience a theory of experience as construct stands revealed as too restrictive a definition of experience. Like Dewey, the notion of experience as construct focuses too exclusively on the how of experience at the expense of the what. Moreover, not every human evaluative response qualifies as a construct. One does not put together artificial sensory experiences or spontaneous emotional responses. Self-controlled thinking, whether intuitive or rational, does exhibit a mediated, constructed character; but we can test the applicability and adequacy of such constructs against the realities that stand within experience. They make us present to those realities in a particular way, some applicable and adequate, others not. Any notion of experience which would present it as a pure construction of the subjective mind would, of course, fall into the fallacy of Kantian subjectivism and solipsism.

In speaking of experience as intentional, Schner alludes to a broad range of philosophical accounts of experience that acknowledge that experience always has a meaningful reference: in other words, one always has an experience **of** something.[4] A triadic construct of experience takes account of an intentional dimension within experience, but it refuses to reduce experience to mere intentional reference. A triadic construct insists that experienced realities stand within experience and not outside of it. Any philosophical construct of experience that would reduce it to mere intentionality would sacrifice the what of experience to the how.

Schner also speaks of experience as derivative. By that he means that schooling, education, and socialization into groups with traditional ways of responding to reality all shape human experience. Moreover, he correctly notes that such received wisdom can never claim uniqueness, irreducibility, or exemption from critique. By portraying experience as fundamentally social, a triadic construct of experience takes this dimension of experience into account.

By experience as dialectical, Schner means that it develops, changes, displaces or transcends itself, and invents new ways of perceiving and acting. By portraying experience as a self-creative process, a triadic construct of experience also takes into account this dimension of experience.

Finally, Schner reflects on two common philosophical uses of the term "experience." First, he questions the legitimacy of any appeal to "common human experience" when such an appeal claims to discover either specific operations common to all humans or a universal content or structure to human experience. While claiming to describe experience, such appeals actually prescribe the way experience must develop. As we have already seen, Rahner's turn to experience falls victim to this fallacy.

Second, Schner reflects on the meaning of the term "religious experience." He distinguishes two common meanings of the term. It can mean the experience of the constitutive elements of a specific religion, or it can refer to a specific dimension of experience.

A triadic construct of experience would acknowledge both uses of the term "religious experience" as legitimate. Moreover, a triadic construct of experience would argue that experience acquires a religious dimension when it becomes tinged with moral absoluteness and ultimacy. Experience acquires moral ultimacy when one commits oneself to values and realities not only worth living for but, if necessary, worth dying for. Experience acquires moral absoluteness when one acknowledges that ultimate values and realities lay claim upon one in all circumstances.

In other words, experience acquires a religious character through moral commitment. Since, however, moral conversion, both personal and socio-political, can occur independently of religious conversion, not every religious experience need have a theistic dimension. It acquires that dimension when one identifies the morally ultimate and the morally absolute as God. One does that when one responds in faith to an encounter with the divine.

I have been arguing in this section of this chapter that a triadic construct of experience gives good promise of conceptual adequacy. By conceptual adequacy I mean the ability to take into account the insights and concerns of other philosophical constructs of experience at the same time that it corrects their limitations and oversights.

But does a triadic construct of experience also enjoy interpretative applicability and adequacy? The terms of an interpretatively applicable construct of experience will apply to some realities as defined. The terms of an interpretatively adequate construct of experience will encounter no realities to which it does not apply. These issues will occupy us in the two sections that follow.

(III)

I have endorsed the methodological principle espoused by both Lonergan and Piaget, that the investigation of experience ought to proceed along multi-disciplinary lines. That means in the first instance that any philosophical construct of experience needs to display the capacity to interpret the results of natural sciences other than philosophy that investigate the development of experience. In writing **Experiencing God** and in subsequent writings, I have attempted to test the capacity of a triadic construct of experience to do precisely that.

I find myself encouraged by the results of this ongoing experiment. I have tested a realistic, social, triadic construct of experience against the results of clinical, empirical, and social psychology. I have also tested it against the results of sociology, comparative religion, and political theory. To date I have encountered no reality for which it cannot account.

Moreover, in the process of this investigation I have recognized that, when one approaches philosophy with contrite fallibilism, the attempt to verify one's philosophical hypothesis in the results of other sciences sets up a dynamic interplay among them.[5]

When one seeks to verify a philosophical hypothesis in the results of other sciences that study the higher forms of experience, one faces four logical possibilities. The philosophical categories and the scientific categories will agree, disagree, converge, or complement one another.

They will agree when they assert fundamentally the same thing about the same reality. They will converge when they say true but different things about the same reality. They will complement one another when they say true things about two different but interrelated realities. They disagree when they say contradictory things about the same reality.

When sets of categories contradict one another one needs to resolve the contradiction by dialectical reversal. One reverses a contradiction dialectically in one of three ways. 1) One endorses one set of categories as true and rejects the other as false. 2) One endorses one set of categories as providing a more adequate frame of reference for understanding the realities under investigation, and one discards the other. 3) One creates a frame of reference more adequate than either of those that contradict one another and integrates into the new frame of reference the best insights of the other two.

For example, when I compared the triadic construct of experience sketched above with the results of developmental psychology I found fundamental agreement between what I mean by experience and what the developmentalists mean. Piaget recognizes intuitive insight into reality and calls it "transductive thinking." He also recognizes the reality of inferential thinking. He recognizes the organic basis of human experience as well as its transactional character. Moreover, besides acknowledging the role of action and of value in experience, Piaget's term "schema" corresponds to what I mean by tendency.

I soon recognized, however, that Piaget's close, empirical exploration of human experience had the capacity to expand my philosophical construct of experience. While my philosophical construct had correctly distinguished between intuitive and inferential thinking, Piaget forced me to recognize more explicitly than I had before that the continuum of conceptual responses that I had named philosophically develops in predictable stages.

For almost two years, infants lack the capacity to image a world and grasp reality through feeling, memory, and sensation. Before young people can reason abstractly, they must learn to reason concretely. Piaget expanded my philosophical insight into experience because what he said about experience and what I said complemented one another. At one level we were saying the same thing about experience, at another level our insights converged. We were saying true but different things about the same reality. Convergent insights amplify one another.

At the same time, I saw that my philosophical construct of experience helped me contextualize the results of focused scientific investigations of human experience. For example, because my triadic construct of experience attempted to describe the whole gamut of human evaluative responses, it provided an over-arching context for identifying which realm of experience any given developmental psychologist had chosen to investigate.

My philosophical construct had recognized the reality of feelings in the development of experience. Erik Erikson offered a plausible account of stages of emotional development. My construct of experience recognized both the intuitive and rational grasp of the real. Piaget's studies of cognitive development gave me a developmental account of how intuitive and rational thinking develop. I recognized moral thinking as a distinct realm of human evaluative response. The work of Charles Kohlberg and other moral developmentalists focused on this realm of experience. James Fowler focused on the religious dimensions of experience.

Moreover, the philosophical contextualization of these different developmental theories enabled me to recognize that on the whole they complemented rather than contradicted one another. They complemented one another because they focused on different, but interrelated, realms of human experience.

Some contradictions did, of course, emerge. Kohlberg and Piaget, for example, offered contradictory accounts of the first two stages of moral development. Piaget describes a child at the first stage of moral development as a young authoritarian; Kohlberg, as an innocently egocentric narcissist. Piaget describes the child at stage two as a democratized authoritarian; Kohlberg, as a socialized narcissist. I suspect, but cannot prove, that a more comprehensive theory of moral development than either Piaget's or Kohlberg's might well validate the insights of both men.

Moreover, I also recognized that my philosophical construct of experience allowed me to put clinical psychology into dialogue with developmental theory. Piaget, for example, recognizes the reality of intuitive, or "transductive," thinking. Jungian archetypal theory discovers recurring, organizing patterns in transductive thinking and names them archetypes.

As I tested my philosophical construct of experience against the results of social psychology, sociology, and political theory, I again found that it could indeed interpret the results of these sciences as well. I saw that not only did a triadic, social construct of experience take account of the kinds of realities that preoccupied these sciences but that the category of tendency, or habit, held the key to understanding human institutional structures. Institutions develop when habitual patterns of behavior enjoy public acknowledgement and sanction in a given community.

I have reflected on these matters in greater detail elsewhere. Here I mention them as evidence that a realistic, social, triadic construct of experience gives promise of interpretative applicability and adequacy.

(IV)

In any interdisciplinary investigation of human experience, one must test the interpretative adequacy of a world hypothesis not only against the results of natural, positive science but also against the results of theological reflection as well.

Frank Schner, in the same article to which I referred above, discovers four major appeals to experience in contemporary theology: the appeal transcendental, the appeal hermeneutical, the appeal constructive, and the appeal confessional. Once again, it seems to me that a realistic, triadic, communal construct of experience can deal with each of these appeals.

The preceding chapter has already reflected in some detail on the appeal transcendental.[6] That appeal correctly discovers within human experience the experience of religious transcendence; but it errs when it tries to build that experience into the **a priori** structure of the human spirit. In a triadic construct of experience, one encounters transcendence by encountering God.

Natural forces have the power to act efficaciously upon us, and we have the capacity to interpret them. When we interpret them accurately we become present to them and they to us. When we misinterpret them, we treat them as though they were something other than what they are. When God touches us efficaciously, we experience that as well and feel ourselves in contact with a force or power that transcends ordinary natural human experiences. When we respond to God in faith, we acknowledge the divine touch for what it is. When we respond in unbelief, we either deny that God has touched us at all; or else, because we find it difficult to deny the fact of a conscious encounter with the Holy, we try to explain away the divine touch as stemming from purely natural causes. If we deny in principle the possibility of a divine touch, we shall almost certainly misconstrue it if and when it happens. Pop psychology, for example, offers a common rationalization in this culture for trivializing and ignoring religious experiences.

Schner contrasts the appeal transcendental with the appeal hermeneutical. The former tries to establish a necessary, universal, **a priori** experience of transcendence. The appeal heremeutical approaches the experience of transcendence with an attitude of suspicion. It stresses the dialectical and functional character of religious faith and, in Schner's judgment, ends in religious skepticism. When the appeal hermeneutical acknowledges religious traditions it relativizes them and the religious appeal that they make.[7]

A triadic construct of experience acknowledges the interpreted character of human experience; but instead of imagining human evaluative responses as barriers between the mind and reality, a triadic construct of experience recognizes that through evaluation and interpretation we become present to our world and it to us. Moreover, a triadic construct of experience recognizes the human mind's self-critical ability to develop norms for distinguishing between sound and unsound evaluations and interpretations of the real.

The same applies to any encounter with the divine. One cannot respond in faith to the divine touch without some prior concept of God. One might acknowledge the uncanny character of an encounter with the Holy; but without religious categories one cannot respond to God as God. The response of faith does not, however, stand as a barrier between the believer and God. On the contrary, it makes the believer consciously present to God. The commitment of faith establishes a developing relationship with God that usually forces the revision of one's original assumptions about God.

In other words, a triadic construct of experience endorses the main lines of what Schner calls the appeal constructive. It avoids the fallacies both of **a priori** argumentation and of relativism. With the appeal constructive, a triadic construct of experience portrays religious experience as "a form of encounter...recognized for its characteristics as constructed, intentional, derivative, and dialectical."[8] In a triadic construct of experience, the certitude of faith derives from the fact that one who has been touched by God and recognized that touch cannot deny its reality. The fallibility of religious belief emerges in the human attempt to interpret the source and consequences of that touch. Its derivative character flows from the fact that in all authentic religious experience God holds the initiative and from the fact that one ordinarily derives one's religious categories from one's culture. The dialectical character of the appeal constructive results from the fact that not everyone interprets religious experience in the same way. Its intentional character flows from the fact that the divine touch invites a conscious human response. Its constructed character results from the fact that the human mind needs symbols to interpret and communicate its encounter with the divine. The response of faith creates the habit of faith; the need to interpret that response correctly creates religious traditions.

Schner correctly recognizes the compatibility between what he calls the appeal constructive and the appeal confessional. While the appeal confessional can degenerate into fundamentalism, it correctly looks to the traditions of religious communities to mediate access to the divine.[9] In order to maintain critical honesty, however, the appeal confessional needs to develop other means for dealing with religious disagreement than the appeal to authority. In my judgment, to date Lonergan's theory of method, when grounded in a sound epistemology, offers the best hope for dealing with the diversity of religious beliefs.

A triadic construct of experience also allows for what Schner calls "the appeal mystical"[10] as long as one does not overdo its apophatic character or portray it as purely subjective. The finitude of the human mind makes any encounter with a supremely intelligible reality mysterious. Only an intelligible God can reveal himself in space and time. A God so absolutely mysterious as to defy all conceptualization, like the One of neo-Platonic mysticism, dwells in eternal and unrevealable solitude. For Christians, then, the fact of the incarnation entails the revealability and therefore the intelligibility of God. The mystery of God results not from divine unintelligibility but from the divine incomprehensibility. We can grasp aspects of the ultimately incomprehensible, but we cannot wrap the whole of our minds around it, no matter how hard we try. As a consequence, no matter how much we learn about God we still have infinitely more to discover.

A triadic construct of experience recognizes, however, the fact of Christian mysticism. When through the cultivation of prayer, loving becomes the primary way of knowing God, then knowledge of the divine advances beyond knowledge mediated by image and concept, which may or may not unite one to God. Serious sinners know God and tremble. The knowing that is loving, however, always unites the mystic to God. Moreover, the Christian mystical tradition discovers degrees of conscious union within mystical prayer.

A survey of some of the principal theological constructs of experience reveals, then, that a triadic construct of experience promises to correct the fallacies of the appeals transcendental and hermeneutical and to incorporate the best insights of the appeals constructive, confessional, and mystical.

Besides testing the adequacy of a triadic construct of experience against major theological models for interpreting religious experience, one needs to test it against Christian revelation itself. Josiah Royce proposed to do precisely that in **The Problem of Christianity.** In that monumental work, he argued that only a metaphysics of community can interpret Christian religious experience. A triadic construct of experience concurs in that insight.

One may, however, question whether Royce's account of the essential ideas of Christianity does full justice to the revelation we have in fact received. Royce identifies those ideas as: 1) only membership in a divine spiritual community mediates salvation, 2) the human individual lives under an inescapable and overwhelming moral burden, and 3) only atonement for sin can release an individual from that burden.[11]

Royce certainly put his finger on three fundamental Christian beliefs; but his account of Christianity has relatively little to say about the person and ministry of Jesus and focuses selectively on

Pauline Christianity. In my judgment, Karl Rahner comes closer to an adequate assessment of the fundamental Christian ideas, when he identifies the Trinity, the incarnation, and the Spirit-inspired church as the three fundamental mysteries of Christian faith. Can a triadic construct of experience interpret these three fundamental mysteries?

When I joined the faculty of the Jesuit School of Theology in 1973, I did so with the intent of pursuing an inculturated foundational theology, in Lonergan's sense of that term. By foundational theology, I mean a strictly normative account of Christian conversion. In the course of elaborating such a theology, I soon recognized that a theology of conversion needs to deal with more than just the subject of conversion. It also needs to deal with the way the convert ought to relate to the religious realities encountered in conversion. As a consequence, within foundational theology, one needs to reach a sound understanding of how converts ought to relate affectively, intellectually, morally, and religiously to the triune God, to the incarnate word, and to the church.

I have advanced far enough in the formulation of a systematic foundational theology to feel confident that a triadic construct of experience can in fact interpret all three fundamental Christian mysteries.[12]

In **The Divine Mother: A Trinitarian Theology of the Holy Spirit,** I tackled the most difficult and fundamental of those mysteries: the Trinity. As we have seen, Protestant process theologians tend to espouse some form of Unitarianism, while Joseph Bracken's sincere attempt to formulate an orthodox trinitarian theology within a Whiteheadean frame of reference has questionable success.

On the other hand, a triadic construct of experience does interpret the historical revelation of the triune God. In reflecting on Bracken's work, I criticized it for having failed to identify a clear principle of verification. In **The Divine Mother,** I suggested that trinitarian theology needs to validate any statement it makes about the triune God in the historical missions of Son and Breath that reveal to us the reality of that God. In other words, the missions of the divine persons provide trinitarian speculation with its principle of validation.

In my judgment a triadic construct of experience not only interprets the reality of the Trinity but also validates its interpretation in the historical missions of Son and Breath. The missions reveal the distinction of persons. A social, triadic construct of experience conceives of persons as autonomous selves capable of acting with self-conscious responsibility. The fact that the Father sends both Son and Breath but is not himself sent reveals him as the aboriginal source of the other two persons. The Son's mission by the Father reveals his distinction from the Father. The Breath's mission by Father and Son simultaneously reveals the Breath's distinction from them.

Moreover, Jesus conducts his mission under the illumination and inspiration of the Holy Breath. That fact reveals the Breath as the cognitive link between Father and Son, i.e. as the mind of God. Within the Christian Godhead, therefore, we can speak not only of three distinct selves but of cognitive evaluations analogous to the values that function in the higher forms of created experience.

We can also speak of efficacious action in the Godhead. The fact that the Father and Son both give rise to a divine person within the Godhead reveals that they act with causal efficacy. Moreover, the New Testament uniformly portrays the Father as acting with aboriginal creative or saving efficacy and the Son as acting with saving and creative obediential efficacy. Because the incarnate Word knows the Father's commands through the illumination of the Breath, in obeying the Father the Son also obeys the Breath. The Son, therefore, stands historically revealed as standing in a relationship of obediential efficacy to both Father and Breath. As a divine person equal to both Father and Breath, the Son's obediential relationship to them does not imply his inferiority to them. It does, however, reveal the Son as the person in the Godhead through whom Father and Breath act on things other than God.

The historical revelation of God allows us, then, to identify within the triune God the same three variables as function within the higher forms of created experience: values, actions, and tendencies. We can then conceive of the Christian God as an experience: not, of course, as a finite, spatio-temporal experience, but as the supreme exemplification of experience, as that experience than which none greater can be conceived, as the experience of all experienceable reality. Since, moreover, experienced realities stand within the experience that grasps them, not outside of it, it follows that all reality exists in God.

Moreover, a triadic construct of experience allows one to conceive the unity of the triune God on an analogy with human social experience. Once again, one needs to look for ways of explaining the unity of the Trinity in the historical revelation we have received. In **The Divine Mother,** I argued that one cannot explain plausibly the unity of a complex reality by identifying it with a fourth reality (like a substance) whose essential simplicity makes three other distinct realities into a unity. One can only explain the unity of a complex reality by its internal relational structure. In other words, the key to offering an account of the unity of the Trinity lies in expanding the notional predicates about the Trinity to include not merely relationships of distinction (as the medievals did) but also unitive relationships as well.

Jesus gives us the clearest evidence of how the divine persons relate to one another. Moreover, we find that evidence most clearly revealed in the paschal mystery. In freely giving himself over to death in obedience to the Father, Jesus gave himself totally into the Father's hands. Moreover, he did so under the illumination of the Breath. In giving himself to the Father in obedience, he simultaneously gave himself totally to the Breath as well. In other words, mutual self-donation describes the relationships among the divine persons that unify the Trinity.

Reflection on human social experience reveals that when human persons give themselves to one another in love they grow alike. They share, as a consequence of that gift, a similarity of life. Embodiment prevents humans from giving themselves to one another with the totality that the divine persons do. When the divine persons give themselves to one another, they share an identity, not just a similarity, of divine life.

Moreover, each divine person contributes something distinctive to the shared life of the triune God. Without the Father, Son and Breath would lack divine creative efficacy. Without the Breath Father and Son would lack conscious personal life. Without the Son, the Father and Breath would lack the divine power to act on things outside the Godhead and therefore would lack the power to create. As a consequence, apart from their mutual self-donation, none of the divine persons could exist as fully personal and fully divine without the others. Moreover, the perfection of their mutual self-gift and the perfection with which they share the divine life means that when they act on realities other than God they act as one. That means that apart from the incarnation, an experienced encounter with the Holy One will probably not disclose the triune character of God's inner life. Only the historical missions of the divine persons does that.

These matters require, of course, more detailed argument than the limits of this study permits. I can therefore only refer readers to **The Divine Mother** for a more detailed account of the argument I have just sketched. The sketch should, however, establish the central point I am trying to make: namely, that a triadic construct of experience gives good promise of providing a creative and innovative understanding of the unity and trinity of the Christian God.

A triadic construct of experience also promises to provide a dynamic interpretation of the hypostatic union. If the Son of God stands historically revealed as a principle of obediential efficacy within the Godhead, then Jesus' human experience underwent a different kind of transformation in God from the kind that we experience in faith.

We experience transformation in God through the enlightenment of the divine Breath. The Breath, however, functions within the Godhead, as an interpretative principle, as the divine mind. That means that the Breath transforms us persuasively, not efficaciously. Moreover, in responding to the Breath's invitations, we act with human autonomy.

Because the human experience we call Jesus underwent transformation in a divine principle of obediential efficacy, Jesus acted with divine, rather than with merely human autonomy. We find in Jesus only one principle of autonomy. Jesus experiences an interpersonal relationship with the Father, but he does not experience an interpersonal relationship with the Son. He spoke and acted as God's Son. Because the experience we know as Jesus functioned with a divine efficacy, it functioned with a divine autonomy as well. As a consequence, we experience Jesus as the fully human, finite experience of being a divine person. No other human experience can make that claim.

In other words, a triadic construct of experience not only promises to interpret the central Christian mystery of the Trinity, but it also promises to interpret the mystery of the incarnation as well. Once again, the reader will find a more detailed account of this experiential construct of the hypostatic union in the pages of **The Divine Mother.** I hope, moreover, in the course of the coming year to bring to a close a dialectical investigation into the issues raised by Christology. Once I have completed that investigation, I shall begin to write the foundational Christology that I hope to publish in the not too distant future. To date, however, in the course of a fairly comprehensive study of the development of New Testament and of post-biblical Christology, I have not found any issue in Christology for which a triadic construct of experience cannot provide an orthodox interpretation.

If a realistic, social, triadic construct of experience promises to interpret Trinity and incarnation, can it also interpret the reality of the church? In matters ecclesial, my own foundational thinking languishes in a much more primitive state than in questions of Trinity and of Christology. Nevertheless, my students have correctly discerned in the foundational sacramental theology I have developed a nascent ecclesiology that I hope one day to flesh out.

In **Models of the Church** Avery Dulles has argued that a contemporary ecclesiology needs to deal with five major models. One needs to deal with the church as institution, as community, as sacrament, as herald, and as servant. The work that I have done in sacramental theology has convinced me that a foundational theology that invokes a triadic, realistic, social construct of experience can deal with all of these dimensions of church life in a unified way. In other words, it promises to provide an over-arching frame of reference for dealing with the issues raised by all five of Dulles' models.

The church as community results directly from the conversion experience that gives one access to membership in it; for that conversion commits one to the life of discipleship. Moreover, the life of discipleship demands that one dedicate oneself to creating the kind of community to which Jesus summons his disciples. Jesus calls us to a community of faith which trusts in the Father's providential care and the Breath's providential guidance. Moreover, absolute assurance of the divine love frees the members of any genuine Christian community to share with others the physical supports of their life, because the community looks to God rather than to things as the ultimate source of life. The sharing of bread and of the other physical resources of life in faith creates the Christian community in an initial way.

Jesus, however, also demanded of his followers a certain quality of sharing. Christian sharing must proceed on the basis of need and not of merit alone. As a consequence, the Christian community must reach across the boundaries that separate people from one another and seek to bring into existence a universal community that welcomes sinners, the marginal, the outcast with the same love as Jesus did.

The life of discipleship also demands that Christian sharing express mutual forgiveness in the image of Jesus, who died forgiving even his murderers. Moreover, in the Christian community, mutual forgiveness tests the authenticity of prayer.

The life of Christian discipleship also includes the sharing of the charisms in community. The divine Breath that dwelt in Jesus in plentitude has been diffused throughout the church, with the result that the church's corporate witness to Christ requires the ongoing interplay of all the charisms within the church. Woe to church bureaucrats who stifle those charisms, for they must face the judgment of God!

Clearly, the life of discipleship not only creates the church as a community, but it also transforms it into a community of mutual service. That service does not restrict itself only to other members of the community but extends in principle to anyone in need. Moreover, as Luke's Pentecost account makes clear, the charismatic action of the divine Breath in the church transforms it into a prophetic community and thus makes it into the herald of Christ.

In the course of developing a sacramental theology, I have argued all of the above points in considerable detail and have, moreover, invoked a triadic, social construct of experience in order to do so. That construct offers a sacramental account of the church because it conceives experience, and therefore all reality, as inherently symbolic.

A triadic account of experience defines a real symbol as any reality that mediates the grasp of meaning. That account acknowledges three generic kinds of symbols: efficacious symbols, interpretative symbols, and communications.

By efficacious symbols I mean physical events, like storms, earthquakes, chemical changes, etc. Events count as symbols because they have a dynamic structure that the human mind can grasp evaluatively. In this sense they mediate the grasp of meaning. Moreover, as we have seen, if people take the time to think clearly about events, then the world will teach us the laws that govern its behavior.

By interpretative symbols, I mean any uncommunicated evaluative response: the sensations, emotions, images, and thoughts that make me present to my world and it to me. Most such responses, of course, exhibit cultural and linguistic conditioning.

By communications I mean efficacious acts that seek to communicate evaluative responses: for example, all speech acts, all artistic activity.

The symbolic structure of human experience takes on a sacramental character in the broad sense of that term, when it undergoes transformation in faith. By a sacrament in the broad sense I mean an event that simultaneously reveals and conceals God. The human response in faith to an encounter with God reveals God by endowing human experience with a transcendent orientation that changes people in ways that manifest the presence of God in their lives. Shared religious experience discloses God more adequately than personal witness; but both reveal the presence of the divine. The transformation of human experience in faith conceals God because no finite reality can manifest the reality of God in a comprehensive way. It can only make some aspect of God present and initially accessible in faith.

Finally, a social, triadic construct of experience promises to interpret the church as institution. That construct, as we have seen, has the categories for dealing with both shared social awareness and with the development of institutional structures within communities. A foundational ecclesiology would, however, need to assess existing church institutions for their capacity to foster all five forms of conversion and their attendant dynamics. Unfortunately, far too many ecclesiastical institutions do nothing of the sort, especially when they have undergone systematic clericalization. Clericalism betrays church leaders into transforming a ministry of service into a power grab that stifles and grieves the Breath of God.

In the course of this book I have been arguing that the turn to experience in contemporary theology has to date produced mixed and often negative results. In the present chapter I have been arguing that it need not. At the basis of the failure of the turn to experience lie two sets of indefensible philosophical assumptions: some form of conceptual nominalism and transcendental Thomism.

Needless to say, a theologian need not make the turn to experience. One might legitimately find another category or set of categories to unify one's theological insights. If, however, one decides to make the turn, then one would be well advised to look into the philosophical and theological advantages of the realistic, triadic, social construct of experience I have presented in this chapter. Moreover, in my judgment, those who make the turn to experience would do well to build on the solid philosophical and theological foundations laid by two giants of the American philosophical tradition: C.S. Peirce and Josiah Royce. Not all may read these geniuses in the same way as I have; but as the preceding analysis suggests, those who make the turn to experience neglect them to their own peril.

Notes

[1] I have developed this construct of experience in other works already cited in this volume: **Experiencing God, The Divine Mother, Grace as**

Transmuted Experience and Social Process, and Inculturating North American Theology. I shall develop it further in a study soon to appear from Liturgical Press called Committed Worship: A Sacramental Theology for Converting Christians.

[2]George P. Schner, S.J., "The Appeal to Experience," Theological Studies (March 1992), vol. 53, no. 1, pp. 40-59.

[3]Ibid., pp. 46-47.

[4]Ibid., pp. 47-48.

[5]The reader will find these matters discussed in considerably more detail in Inculturating North American Theology.

[6]Ibid., p. 52.

[7]Ibid., pp. 53-54.

[8]Ibid., pp. 54-55.

[9]Ibid., pp. 55-56.

[10]Ibid., pp. 57-58.

[11]Josiah Royce, The Problem of Christianity, I, pp. 34-44.

[12]The reader will find both the trinitarian theology here presented and the construct of the hypostatic union that follows it in The Divine Mother.

Index

Philosophers. *See* specific
  names
Philosophy, 2, 3, 14, 17, 53–54,
  109. *See also* American
  philosophy
Piaget, Jean, 96, 101, 124, 143,
  144
Pittenger, W. Norman, 69,
  70–72, 77, 79
Plato, 5–6, 15, 34, 100
Politics, 28, 29, 48, 65
Powers, spiritual, 101, 102
Practice, 26, 28–29, 37, 42
Pragmatic logic, 29–37, 42–43,
  45, 48
Pragmatic maxim, 32–33, 35,
  42–43
Pragmatism
  liberation theology and,
    24–25, 26, 122
  orthodoxy and, 32, 36,
    37–42
  orthopraxis and, 32, 36,
    37–42
  Peirce and, 25, 29–37
Praxis
  Boff and, 28, 29, 54, 55
  experience and, 24
  interpretation and, 11
  liberation theology and,
    24–25, 26, 122
  politics and, 29, 48
  Schillebeeckx and, 10, 11
  theology and, 26, 28, 29
  theory and, 28
Pre–apprehension, 98
Pre–conscious, 135

Predictability, 30, 32, 43, 59
Prehension, 57, 64, 66
Processes, 52–53, 55
Process theology
  Bracken and, 80–81, 81–84
  Christian revelation and, 68,
    69–84
  Cobb and, 73–74
  conceptual nominalism and,
    122
  cosmology of Whitehead
    and, 84
  critical examination of,
    58–69
  emergence of, 69
  evolution of, 69–70
  God and, 62
  Griffin and, 72–73
  nominalism and, 53–58
  philosophy and, 53–54
  Pittenger and, 69, 70–72, 77
  positive aspects of, 52–53
  Protestant, 69–70, 123, 149
  Suchocki and, 74–79
  turn to experience and, 1, 15,
    52–53, 84
  Whitehead and, 52
Protestant process theology,
  69–70, 123, 149
Prudential thought, 116–117,
  128
Psyche, human, 95
Psychology, 44–45, 101–102,
  143–144. *See also*
  Thomistic faculty
  psychology